SPIRITUAL
MATURITY

Other titles in

PRISMS

SPIRITUAL MATURITY

Preserving Congregational Health and Balance

FRANK A. THOMAS

Fortress Press
Minneapolis

SPIRITUAL MATURITY
Preserving Congregational Health and Balance

Cover image: Ashanti weave cloth. Copyright © Planet Art, 2002.
Used by permission
Cover design: Marti Naughton
Book design: Ann Delgehausen

Library of Congress Cataloging-in-Publication Data
Thomas, Frank A.
    Spiritual maturity : preserving congregational health and balance /
Frank A. Thomas.
        p. cm. (Prisms)
    ISBN 0-8006-3086-6 (alk. paper)
        1. Church management. 2. Church controversies. 3. Christian
leadership. I. Title.

BV652 .T52 2002
253—dc21   2002283663

Manufactured in the U.S.A.
06   05   04   03   3   4   5   6   7   8   9   10

Dedicated to the memory and humor of
EDWIN H. FRIEDMAN

CONTENTS

Module 4

PREFACE

What kind of leadership, membership, and following are needed in the Christian church if we are to be effective and relevant for God-centered ministry in the twenty-first century? As we face the challenges of the new millennium, what kind of discipleship is needed to foster a truly dynamic Christian church that is able to faithfully and boldly serve the needs of this present age? My fear is what one of my major mentors taught and believed: that in churches, families, institutions, and nations everywhere, generally the most creative, dynamic, and imaginative people are not the ones who set the agenda and establish direction. Instead the most dependent people—the chronic complainers and the regressive thinkers—set the tone for the response to present and future challenges.

As I have experienced it, the majority of church members will support the vision, move forward in new directions, and mount new vistas, but usually a small minority is able to keep the leaders and the other members at bay. The leaders and the majority of the members spend so much time addressing the grievances of the chronic complainers and attempting to satisfy the regressive elements that they are effectively hindered from accomplishing the mission and the vision of the church. Chronic complainers and whiners draw critical time and energy away from purposeful fulfillment of the mission. The maturity, skill, and ability to disallow chronic complainers and the regressive element to dislodge the church from its mission and vision is what I mean by the title of this book, *Spiritual Maturity: Preserving Congregational Health and Balance.*

This manual on maturity is designed to explore mature Christian leadership, membership, and following. It is designed to provide tools for the church to preserve health and balance in the congregational body and stay on track for its mission and vision. This book attempts to set parameters for mature dissent and disagreement such that opposition does not become chronic and complaining, does not become regressive, thus hindering the mission and the vision of the church. This book is intended not to wipe out opposition or dissent but to set the framework for honestly and forthrightly handling differences of opinion in a mature manner that allows the church to maintain focus. This book is about spiritual and personal maturity that contributes to corporate maturity. Ultimately, it is about taking the focus off other people and choosing responses that foster one's own growth and maturity. In the end, it is not about being a victim but about choosing one's destiny and calling in response to what one has heard from God and permitting others to do the same. This book is about preserving one's personal health and balance in order to help preserve health and balance in the congregational body.

On behalf of my wife, Joyce, my son, Tony, and daughter, Rachel, I express our gratitude and thanks to the many members of the New Faith Baptist Church of Matteson, Illinois, and the Mississippi Boulevard Christian Church of Memphis, Tennessee, who have directly helped us learn to preserve our health and balance. I thank so many of our mentors: Jeremiah Wright Jr., Fredrick G. Sampson III, Henry and Ella Mitchell, Vincent and Rose Harding, Edwin Friedman, Ed Wheeler, and so many others too numerous to name. I thank a classmate from years ago whose list of principles was the seed I have grown into this book. I have been unable to find that classmate's name, but I would like to acknowledge the important influence that our conversations had on my thinking. I also thank Jini Kilgore Ross who so patiently went through the multiple drafts word by word and line by line. We thank our parents, who were our first leaders, John Frank Thomas, Almetha King Thomas, Jannie Rowry Scott, and William Scott Jr.

We give thanks to Almighty God who has so marvelously carried us through joy, mistakes, laughter, pain, victory, tribulation, triumph, and difficulty. If God asked us, we would do it all over again. Finally, we offer this manual in the hope that leaders, members, followers, and we, ourselves, might be healed for the great work that is ours to serve this present age.

INTRODUCTION

Several years ago, I sat in a powerful community of church leaders who were exploring our own spiritual and personal maturity and how to promote spiritual and personal maturity in congregational life. After days of intensive discussion, one of the class members produced a list of twenty-five principles he had developed for his congregation that he believed promoted maturity in the Body of Christ. Outside of the session, I discussed the principles with him in great detail. The principles and the conversation were such an awesome seed of creativity for my ministry and my life that I began to rethink my approach to maturity in congregational life. I realized how long church leaders had neglected to establish a practical, integrated, and holistic standard for maturity in the Body.

Traditionally, when we spoke of indicators of spiritual maturity in the Body, we emphasized the fruit of the Spirit in Galatians 5, the list of qualifications for elders and deacons in 1 Timothy 3 and Acts 6, and the ability to love in 1 Corinthians 13. But there was something exciting about phrasing maturity in a new, different, and complementary way. I came to believe that the way maturity functions in the Body is analogous to how the immune system functions in the physical body—that maturity is the Body's immune system.

Maturity defends against pathological invaders that threaten the spiritual health of the organism. Maturity defines the boundaries of the organism, distinguishing and killing alien threats, and repairing any part of the organism that has been damaged. In other words, maturity mounts a spiritual defense and repairs the emotional damage of the Body.

I have been a pastor for twenty-two years, and because I have found the work difficult, demanding, and challenging, the development of my maturity was a significant step in increasing my level of satisfaction, fulfillment, and contentment in the pastoral role. Recently, I went

1

to lunch with a rabbi friend, and he passionately and poignantly articulated his belief that congregational leadership was damaging to one's body and soul. I immediately chimed in with agreement, and we listed some of the pitfalls that made congregational leadership dangerous to one's spiritual, physical, and emotional health. We recognized that it is possible for pastors or rabbis to be worship leaders and so regularly meet the needs of others in worship that they rarely have the opportunity to be worshipers themselves. We recognized that when one teaches prayer and Bible as consistent and regular parts of one's work all day, many times the last things that one feels like doing at home are prayer and Bible devotions. We acknowledged compassion fatigue, the irrepressible exhaustion that comes from being compassionately and regularly available to the needs of people. We acknowledged the deep and agonizing pain that goes with the inevitable conflicts that arise, the emotionally draining mountaintop highs, and the dismal valley lows that come often within the same hour or day in the normal flow of congregational life. And because it was so painful, we could only barely mention the gargantuan stress on family life from the long hours and the unrealistic expectations.

In general, we concluded that one could be so busy working for God that one could lose his or her relationship with God. We concluded that the only way to redeem the damaging nature of the clergy position is to operate from the mature perspective that one's service to God through the congregation is an opportunity to discover and develop what one deeply believes about God, life, and the world. We concluded that traveling the road of maturity involved spending less time complaining about the difficulty of the position, and more time taking responsibility for our healthy and unhealthy responses. I concluded that maturity functions as the immune system does to repair and protect the damaged body and soul from the hazards of the clergy life.

Edwin H. Friedman in his classic work, *Generation to Generation: Family Process in Church and Synagogue,* suggests that congregational leadership can be a "healing modality."[1] I have come to understand him to mean that if a leader can treat his or her transitions and crises as opportunities for growth, rather than hostile experiences that victimize and require escape, then the leader will increase his or her level of spiritual and personal maturity. And when the leader has increased his or her personal maturity, then leadership is a healing modality. I am thankful that I have come closer to the place that my experiences in congregational life are opportunities for growth.

Following the excellent model of my aforementioned class member, I conceived of maturity as a series of concrete principles. I established practical statements that reflect values and principles that cultivate the spiritual, personal, and corporate growth and maturity necessary for the church to accomplish its mission and vision. I developed the "Statement of Health, Balance, and Maturity in Congregational Life," which is a set of principles that pinpoint a vision of what maturity looks like in congregational life. This book was written to explore the lessons and principles of my Statement, and explain their practical application to congregational life. The "Statement of Health, Balance, and Maturity in Congregational Life" is included in its entirety in the appendix on page 91 of this book.

The starting point for any Christian maturity is a saving relationship with Jesus Christ that I call the Victorious Christian Life (Module 1: The Call to the Victorious Christian Life). Once the saving relationship is established, then we must ascertain and develop our personal maturity because on the basis of our personal maturity we engage the world and relationships with others (Module 2: The Mature Self). After discerning our maturity, then we must test and build up our maturity in the midst of a church community (Module 3. The Mature Church Member). If we build our maturity to a certain point, then we are ready to become church leaders (Module 4: The Mature Church Leader). We close the book with concluding ideas and summation that include insights for further thinking and clarification in the epilogue.

I wrote *Spiritual Maturity* to help the church redefine health and disease in the congregational body, and empower individuals with responsibility, more control, and more freedom in their lives. For example, when an important giver calls to announce that if the church makes a certain decision that he or she will withdraw his or her funds, the leader might combat the closed in feeling by consulting the fifth principle of Module 3: I believe the withdrawal of financial, spiritual, or physical participation and support, but not membership, to protest a pastoral, leadership, or congregational decision is an abuse of the privilege of participation.

It is my hope that these principles of maturity will give readers the power to make a difference in the state of their own health.

THE CALL TO THE VICTORIOUS CHRISTIAN LIFE

If we would preserve health and balance in the congregational body, then we must first understand what fundamental difference an experience of Christ makes in the lives we live in this world. Jesus Christ gives to each person for whom he is Savior a Victorious Christian Life (VCL). We must understand what a VCL looks like, and the characteristics that would immediately identify one as a victor in Christ.

Lesson 1:
The Call to the VCL—John 16:33

THE CHURCH IS THE PLACE WHERE PEOPLE CAN HEAR CHRIST
URGE THEM TO A VICTORIOUS CHRISTIAN LIFE.

"I have told you these things, so that in me you may have peace. In this world you will have trouble. But take heart! I have overcome the world."
—John 16:33

Biblical scholars have traditionally labeled chapters 14–17 of the Gospel of John as the Farewell Discourses of Jesus. In these chapters, Jesus attempts to prepare the disciples for the completion of his work on the earth and his victorious return to God. He comforts his disciples when they find themselves confused and grieved over his announcement that he will leave them. Jesus explains to them the heavenly plan that is behind what is about to occur in Jerusalem. He foretells his persecution and the similar persecution that they, his disciples, will suffer. He promises that the Holy Spirit, the Spirit of Truth, will be with them forever to teach and guide them into all truth.

Jesus spends a tremendous amount of time teaching about the role of the Holy Spirit. The disciples finally begin to indicate that they understand his teachings and beliefs, and Jesus reassures them that he has told them all these things so they might have peace. Despite everything that can and will happen, including arrest, crucifixion, and death, they can be confident because they will experience resurrection, healing, and peace. In John 16:33, Jesus establishes one of the foundational scriptures for the VCL when he says to the grieving disciples, "In this world, you will have tribulation. But be of good cheer! I have overcome the world."

Jesus is very clear that we will have tribulation in this world. He teaches that one of the fundamental truths of this world is that tragedy is available for everyone, even Christians. God did not say in Gen. 1:31 that the world was perfect, but rather that the world was good, so suffering is a part of the matrix of human experience. People will get crippling diseases, suffer stillborn births, and experience layoffs, cancer, drug addictions, murder, rape, persecutions, racism, social and economic inequity, political arrest, torture, drive-by shootings, war, and death. Even if one is a Christian, there is a good possibility that one will experience at least some of these things. But even given these terrible and painful realities, everyone who has established a relationship with Jesus Christ as Savior will still be victorious because Christ has overcome the world. In his resurrection from death, Christ has overcome this world and all of its available tragedy, thus assuring us a VCL. This promise and present reality of overcoming the world's trials and tribulations are what we call a VCL. As the family of Jesus Christ, therefore, we can be of good cheer because we have all the benefits of the resurrection—a VCL.

The Church is the coming together of those who have received a VCL to celebrate and strengthen their experience of victory in Christ but, also, to extend to others the invitation to receive a VCL. The Church is the gathering of redeemed people that helps Christ urge others to receive the full benefit of a VCL. The world is full of people who are experiencing life's tragedies without the help, comfort, or assurance of victory, and who would receive untold benefit from the VCL. It is the role of the church to extend the victory of Jesus to the world. It is the mission of the church to share the VCL with all who would receive it.

Lesson 2:
The Few, the Proud, the Victorious—
Matt. 7:13-14

JESUS SAYS THAT THE WAY LEADING TO DESTRUCTION IS BROAD
AND EASY, AND THERE ARE MANY WHO FIND IT. THE WAY THAT
LEADS TO A VCL IS NARROW AND HARD, AND THERE ARE FEW
WHO FIND IT AND POSSESS IT.

*"Enter through the narrow gate. For wide is the gate and broad
is the road that leads to destruction, and many enter through
it. But small is the gate and narrow the road that leads to life,
and only a few find it."*

—Matt. 7:13-14

A mantra from a recruiting advertisement for the United States Marine Corps
boasts, "The Few, The Proud, The Marines." The ad features an im-
maculately dressed, fully decorated Marine in complete uniform
with a sword at his side. As the camera circles the entire circumfer-
ence of the faultless marine, the image vividly communicates the
message that Marines are lean, mean, and disciplined fighting ma-
chines. It is clear from the ad that only a very select group that is
highly tested, trained, and skilled—the few and the proud—can become Marines. I believe Jesus when he says the way that leads to life
(VCL) is narrow and hard, and there are few that find it. I believe
overcoming Christians are The Few, The Proud, The Victorious.

In Matt. 7:13-14, Jesus illustrates the difficulty of the VCL by encouraging believers to enter through the narrow gate. Jesus paints the
picture of a narrow gate and a wide gate. The wide gate and its ac-
companying wide road both lead to destruction. Many people will
enter through the wide gate and travel the wide road to destruction.
But there is a narrow gate with a narrow road, and they both lead to
life (VCL). Jesus encourages us to go through the narrow gate to the
narrow road that leads to the VCL. There are only a few who find the
narrow gate. The Few. The Proud. The Victorious.

The VCL is the narrow and the hard way. On the surface, we all
would like to receive it, but we have to work to truly possess it. A
VCL sounds and feels good, and probably not many Christians

would balk at the opportunity to receive one, but receiving it and possessing it are two different things. While God makes the VCL available, one has to work on and within oneself to truly possess the VCL. The gate is narrow because many of us find it extremely difficult to do the hard work to possess our victory in Christ; we find it extremely difficult to grow and become mature. There is no harder work in life than growing and becoming mature, and that is the work that is absolutely necessary to fully possess our VCL.

In giving us the VCL, God has given us the power to mature and become whole. The VCL gives us the power to make the necessary changes in our lives to become free and mature. On the one hand, my experience is that through faith and surrender to God, God works in and through me to bring me to maturity. On the other hand, the temptation is to assume that God can change and mature us without any real work or effort on our part. I get all tangled up and defeated when the effort is solely mine and conclude, as Paul, "Woe is me! Who shall deliver me from this body of death?" We must find the delicate balance where God works and we consent to the work of God; where God changes, but we do all in our own power to change; where we give God the glory for maturity, but we take responsibility for our part of the effort to get there. We have the VCL, but we must take responsibility for our part in the effort to truly possess it.

In a book called, *Passionate Marriage,* David Schnarch points out that the downfall of many relationships is that we are always looking for the right person. It never dawns on us to become the right person, or to understand that this difficult person we are unsure about might be in our lives to help facilitate grinding off our rough edges so we might become the right person. Schnarch quotes Hugh and Gayle Prather "Did I pick the right person? This question inverts the starting and ending points. We do not pick our perfect match because we ourselves are not perfect. The universe hands us a flawless diamond in the rough. Only if we are willing to polish off every part of ourselves that cannot join do we end up with a soul mate."[1]

The wide gate that leads to destruction is to continually look for the right person and delude ourselves into believing that when we find the right person, job, house, car, church, etc., then we will be happy. This is the human tendency to look outside of ourselves for peace, contentment, fulfillment, and joy, and to believe that something or someone can make us happy. If Christ is our Savior, ultimate peace, joy, and contentment are found within ourselves, in our relationship with God, and in our courage to live out our deepest beliefs and values.

It is only when we polish off every part of ourselves that cannot join that we will find relationships and life truly meaningful and fulfilling. But polishing ourselves and discovering ourselves is hard work, the hardest work of life. The narrow gate is for those who allow Christ to mold and shape them into the right person. The narrow gate is doing the emotional, spiritual, experiential, and intellectual work to possess the VCL, and thereby discovering what one truly and deeply believes, and living it out before the world without the need for approval or validation. People who do this work in Christ are able to possess and enjoy a VCL. They are The Few. The Proud. The Victorious.

Lesson 3:
Overcoming the Fear of Freedom—
John 1:12-13

THE BASIS OF A VCL IS NOT FREEDOM AS A SOCIAL, ECONOMIC, OR POLITICAL CATEGORY BUT FREEDOM AS AN INNER SPIRITUAL REALITY AND IDENTITY THAT IS BASED ON A SAVING RELATIONSHIP WITH CHRIST.

WE ARE 100 PERCENT RESPONSIBLE FOR MAINTAINING THE FREEDOM OF A VCL BASED ON HOW WE RESPOND TO THE EVENTS, SITUATIONS, AND CIRCUMSTANCES THAT OCCUR IN OUR LIVES.

ONE WHO HAS THE FREEDOM OF A VCL GRANTS TO OTHERS THE FREEDOM TO BE 100 PERCENT RESPONSIBLE FOR HOW THEY RESPOND TO THE EVENTS, SITUATIONS, AND CIRCUMSTANCES OF THEIR LIVES.

Yet to all who received him, to those who believed in his name, he gave the right to become children of God—children born not of natural descent, nor of human decision or a husband's will, but born of God.

—John 1:12-13

At its core, I believe the VCL is about the freedom that Christ gives every believer. Some believe that freedom is a political, social, or economic category that one group of people bestows upon another. According to this thinking, America and Abraham Lincoln "gave" African Americans their freedom with the Emancipation Proclamation and the hard-fought concessions and gains made in the Civil Rights Movement during the 1950s and 1960s. African Americans marched, picketed, boycotted, preached, prayed, sang, and engaged in social protest to "get" their freedom. I believe African Americans did not engage in social protest to become free. I believe they engaged in social protest because they were free and would not allow anyone to enslave them.

The first principle of VCL is, *freedom is an inner spiritual reality and identity given by Christ from which social, economic, and political rights, responsibilities, and freedoms flow.* Freedom at its core is the spiritual reality and identity that Jesus Christ bestows upon everyone who believes in him. The writer of the Gospel of John speaks of this freedom when he says in 1:12-13 and 8:36, "To all who believed in his name, he gave the right to become the children of God; children born not of natural descent, nor of human decision, or a husband's will, but born of God. . . . So if the Son sets you free, you will be free indeed."

Jesus has given us the right to become children of God, and thereby sets the sons and daughters of God free. It is not a freedom born of constitutional right or human decision or the will of a court, but a freedom and identity given by God through Christ. The social protest marches of the sixties were not undertaken to generate freedom, but happened because many people with roots in the church were already free in Christ, and refused to accept slavery or segregation. The freedom that Christ gives is the first and core principle of the VCL.

If freedom in Christ is the essential characteristic of the VCL, then nothing can defeat us: death cannot hold us, and the grave cannot keep us; enemies cannot kill us, and violence cannot overcome us; hate cannot make us bitter, and tribulations cannot make us give up. We are free and victorious over all things, such as cancer, divorce, sickness, disease, institutional racism, murder, violence, and substance abuse. Based on the death and the resurrection of Jesus Christ, we are victorious over evil, whatever its shape, form, or manifestation.

While we are free at our Christian birth, our most difficult task following our rebirth in Christ is to take hold of our freedom and possess it by appropriating it concretely and maturely in this life. Taking hold of and possessing our freedom means that we have the choice to respond to every circumstance from within the authority of our freedom. We can choose fear, worry, doubt, hate, and other negatives as responses to events or circumstances that we encounter, but they are inconsistent with our freedom and rob us of it. We can, out of our freedom, choose love, peace, healing, and positive attitudes and actions as our response to absolutely every circumstance of life. This is the heart of the VCL—to exercise the freedom to choose positive responses to any situation in life because the Son has set us free indeed. The victory is already ours, so we have no reason to respond with hate, fear, or fret. This leads us to the second major characteristic of the VCL: *we are responsible for maintaining our freedom based on how we respond to life.*

Gary Gore, the founder of a marvelous teamwork ministry called Team Trek, teaches that we are 100 percent responsible for how we respond to the people, events, and circumstances of our lives. We are not 100 percent responsible for what happens to us, but we are 100 percent responsible for how we respond to what happens to us. We have victory in Christ, and in every event or circumstance of life we have the choice to respond in ways that are consistent with our belief that we are free, and therefore cannot be defeated. But when we choose bitterness, hate, envy, or other negative responses, we must ask if we have truly taken hold of our freedom in Christ. Do we *believe* that we are free?

The things that happen to us in this life provide the occasion and choice for us to define ourselves and what we believe through our "response-ability"—our ability to respond. Circumstances are nothing but the opportunity for us to gage response-ability from within our freedom given by Christ. Paul gives this same value to response when he says in 1 Thess. 4:13, "Let us not grieve like those who do not have any hope." Paul is entreating the Thessalonians to respond in a manner consistent with their deepest belief about God. God has assured us of the victory in Jesus Christ, and we must let this truth shape how we respond to those who have died. Freedom is the opportunity to build and develop our response-ability. Freedom in Christ shapes every response of the VCL.

If we truly take hold of freedom as the inner spiritual reality and identity bestowed by Christ, and if we live out that freedom, then we must allow others to be free. We are free to respond, and we must allow others the freedom to respond in ways that are consistent with their values and deepest beliefs. If I am 100 percent responsible for how I respond to life, then I must allow others to be 100 percent responsible for their response-ability and choices in life, regardless of whether or not I like, agree with, or support their choices. This is the third principle of the VCL: *the VCL grants others the freedom to be 100 percent responsible for how they respond to the events, situations, and circumstances of their lives.*

The freedom of a VCL does more than tolerate differences, it accepts and respects differences as fundamental to one's own and others' freedom. If we grant others the freedom to respond, they may not make the same choices that we make. This means that there will be differences. If I have the right to choose, then everyone has the right to choose. People do not make the same lifestyle choices, but we must allow people the freedom to make and be responsible for their own choices. People have a right to choose moral values that are different from what we like, agree with, or support, and they also have a responsibility to account for those choices. I believe that one of the surest signs of spiritual maturity and freedom in Christ is our ability to handle differences constructively. How we handle differences with others says a tremendous amount about our own freedom. If we are not careful, we will deny others the right to freedom and choice that we so desperately need and want for ourselves.

Most of us say the politically correct thing—that we like differences—but in our choices of churches, schools, neighborhoods, and lifestyles there is little diversity. We generally find ourselves with people who make about the same choices in life that we do. The truth is that differences are difficult. Differences stretch us and cause us to grow and examine our beliefs. If we would really be open to them, differences would help us to polish off our rough edges.

Our response-ability is not hindered by differences but by the fact that we are anxious about them. Differences are not the problem in our world—how anxious and stressed we become over the differences is the problem. For example, once my wife and I had an argument. Three hours later we talked about it again and settled what we disagreed over. Had anything changed in regard to the differences themselves that would make resolution easier? No! We had calmed down about the differences, and then we could see what principles were behind our positions and how we might move or compromise but still maintain the truth and integrity of our positions. Alternatively, we might have been able to point out that we were wrong, or pinpoint what in our behavior made our differences into an argument. This kind of maturity is response-ability. Freedom in Christ is about this kind of personal response-ability.

In his book *The Greeks and the Irrational* E. R. Dodd suggests that by the third century B.C.E., the Greeks were around the corner from a cultural renaissance. They were close to learning how to take personal responsibility for their choices and were moving to become a free and open society. He suggests that just as they were right there at the edge of freedom, fear of it possessed them, and they returned to superstition. He says they had a massive "failure of nerve," the price of which was 1,000 years of nonenlightenment for Europe known as the Dark Ages. Dodd suggests that whenever there is a failure of nerve and the refusal of responsibility, "there is a price to be paid, usually in the form of neurosis." He states that he does not know why a people would ride to the brink and not jump, wondering whether it was the horse that refused to jump or the rider. He would suggest that the Greeks rode to the brink of freedom but refused to possess it.[2]

I wonder if many Christians are just as guilty as the Greeks. Christ has made freedom possible. We accept Christ and ride right to the brink, and then we must choose whether or not we will jump. We must decide if we will take up the mantle of personal responsibility and choice and be 100 percent responsible for our actions, decisions, and responses. We move in either the direction of freedom or, by our refusal of responsibility, in the direction of neurosis. Gal. 5:1 says, "It is for freedom that Christ has set us free. Stand firm then, and do not let yourselves be burdened again by a yoke of slavery."

THE MATURE SELF

It is very difficult to preserve health and balance in our personal or congregational body without a commitment to personal responsibility. Personal responsibility is a stimulant to the immune system and one of the prime indicators of maturity and health. Without personal responsibility, the personal and congregational body is mired in excuses, blame, anger, and finger pointing, which are the result of disease. The principles discussed in this module represent core beliefs that shape and monitor a commitment to personal responsibility.

Lesson 1:
The Sin of Playing Victim—Gen. 3:1-13

FOLLOWING THE ORIGINAL SIN OF DISOBEDIENCE, THE MOST APPEALING, MOST PREVALENT, AND MOST FREQUENTLY NON-RESISTED TEMPTATION IS TO PLAY THE ROLE OF VICTIM.

And [God] said, "Who told you that you were naked? Have you eaten from the tree that I commanded you not to eat from?"
The man said, "The woman you put here with me—she gave me some fruit from the tree, and I ate it."
Then the Lord God said to the woman, "What is this you have done?"
The woman said, "The serpent deceived me, and I ate."
—Gen 3:11-13

The first principle of this module reflects what I call the sin of playing victim, found in Gen. 3:1-13. For much of interpretative biblical history, biblical scholars have primarily focused on Adam and Eve's sinful act of disobedience in eating what they were commanded not to eat, recorded in Genesis 3. Yet I believe the same passages also clearly illustrate what might be considered the companion of original sin—playing the role of victim. The original sin was not simply the act of disobedience, but the unwillingness of Adam to take responsibility when God confronted him about his behavior. Adam was not willing to take responsibility for his relationship with God and the choices, decisions, and actions that flowed from that relationship. Instead, he and Eve established a disobedience/victim pattern that is basic and fundamental to human nature, reverberating through the ages of human history in various forms and disguises.

Genesis 3 says that the serpent was the craftiest of all the animals, causing Eve to question God's command, and enticing her to eat from the tree of which God commanded her and Adam not to eat. Eve first, and then Adam ate the fruit, and they gained knowledge of their nakedness, sewed fig leaves to hide their exposure, and concealed themselves from God.

The sin of playing victim is seen in Adam's lack of responsibility for his actions. He was responsible for his choice, regardless of Eve's bidding, yet he placed the blame for his choice outside of himself. First, he tried to blame Eve by intimating that she gave him the fruit, and unsuspectingly he ate. In other words, because he did not know what he was doing, he was not really guilty of anything. Then, he even attempted to blame the Lord God by saying that God put the woman in the garden with him, and if God had not put the woman in the garden, then he would not be in this trouble. His response indicates that he did not believe himself to be responsible for his choices. His response is indicative of his belief that he was not a mature moral agent who could make choices to hinder or help his life. *Maturity is defined as the willingness to take responsibility for one's own relationship with God and the life, decisions, choices, and actions that flow from that relationship.* Adam was immature and gave someone else responsibility for his life. The sin of playing victim attempts to shift the blame and responsibility outside of oneself.

Let's look carefully at Eve's response also. God confronted her and asked, "What is this that you have done?" Eve responded, "The serpent deceived me, and I ate." Actually, she did better at being responsible than did Adam. At least she stated the facts: the serpent deceived her, and she ate. At least she admitted that she was deceived, and indicated her responsibility in her culpability. She did not try to place the blame anywhere else. Her sin was primarily disobedience, and Adam's sin was disobedience and playing victim. Maybe the human problem of evil and sin can be summed up in the action and response of this couple to God's commands. Human beings disobey like Adam and Eve, and they deny and place blame like Adam.

ANY STATEMENT THAT BEGINS WITH "HE/SHE/YOU/IT MADE ME . . ." REFLECTS THE TEMPTATION TO PLAY VICTIM.

That statement is a reliable and practical litmus test for recognizing victim thinking whenever it arises in my life. Victim thinking is placing blame or responsibility for my actions outside of myself. People engaged in victim thinking say things like, "She made me feel inferior," or "He made me feel shame." No one can "make" a person feel anything without the complicity and consent of the person doing the feeling.

I must continually remind myself that no one makes me feel or do anything. If I feel or do anything it is because of my choice and my decision. No one makes me sad. I choose to be sad in response to my own actions or the actions of someone else. For example, our family recently moved to Memphis, Tennessee. No one forced us to move to Memphis, but we chose to do so based on our understanding of God's will for our lives. Our move has been made infinitely easier by the constant reminder that we chose to be here. We chose to respond to God's will for our lives. It has helped us during the painful points of transition not to allow ourselves to play the victim role. We take responsibility for our relationship with God and the life, decisions, choices, and actions that flow from that relationship. Anything less than this is the sin of victim thinking.

In my deliberation on the sin of victim thinking, I considered the possibility of legitimate victims in the world. I did not want it misconstrued that I believed that there were/are no legitimate victims. In other words, what is the sin? Is being a victim a sin? Or is playing a victim a sin? There are legitimate victims in the world, such as children who suffer sexual, physical, or psychological abuse. Children are learning response-ability, and therefore are not as able as adults to take responsibility for their emotional well-being. Children can be legitimate victims, and being this kind of victim is not a sin.

There are also victims in the actions of rape, murder, slavery, and genocide, among others, where evil was perpetrated against a person or group. Some of these persons are victims of what Walter Wink calls "natal alienation."

[T]here is such a thing as "natal alienation," . . . the experience of being born into a world in which one is condemned in advance, by virtue of one's skin color, or gender, or disability, or malnutrition, or a mother's addiction, or AIDS, to a future more or less blocked off. We are not talking about just an occasional aberration but about hundreds of millions of people. If South African "Bantu education" has been intentionally geared to teach just enough to train blacks for work in the mines, but not enough for them to achieve competitive parity with whites, how free are they to "be all that they can be" under God?[1]

Adults more than children have the ability to take responsibility for their emotional well-being even after an evil act has been perpetrated against them. Primarily, the sin of playing victim has to do with a response after an initial action of disobedience, but also the unwillingness of adults to be responsible for their emotional well-being in the aftermath of a violent act, people being unwilling to be responsible for the quality of their life in general. There is no sin in being a victim. The sin is in playing a victim.

Lesson 2:
The Sin of Playing Savior—Luke 15:11-27

FOLLOWING THE SIN OF PLAYING VICTIM, THE MOST APPEALING, MOST PREVALENT, AND MOST FREQUENTLY NONRESISTED TEMPTATION IS TO PLAY THE ROLE OF SAVIOR.

"So he got up and went to his father.
"But while he was still a long way off, his father saw him and was filled with compassion for him; he ran to his son, threw his arms around him and kissed him.
"The son said to him, 'Father, I have sinned against heaven and against you. I am no longer worthy to be called your son.'
"But the father said to his servants, 'Quick! Bring the best robe and put it on him. Put a ring on his finger and sandals on his feet. Bring the fattened calf and kill it. Let's have a feast and celebrate. For this son of mine was dead and is alive again; he was lost and is found.' So they began to celebrate."
—Luke 15:20-24

Playing savior is the determination to seize from other people or institutions their responsibility for their choices, actions, and decisions. To play savior is to grab responsibility away from another by taking it up as one's own. *Playing savior is to do for others what they can do for themselves.*

Playing savior, or hero, reflects the belief that other persons are not able to, and cannot or will not take responsibility for their own lives—therefore, we must do it for them. We take over people's lives and rescue people and institutions from the responsibility that goes with their actions, choices, and decisions. Although we think we can exhibit great nobility and heroism when we play savior, taking responsibility from another is still sin. A very critical aspect of playing savior is that we do not allow people to experience the consequences of their behaviors. We rescue people from their consequences.

We must acknowledge that the world has one savior—Jesus Christ. Jesus by his death, burial, and resurrection, delivered us from the consequences of sin (Rom. 6:23). Jesus did for us what we could not do for ourselves. Regardless of whatever we might try, we cannot reverse the disobedience/victim pattern of Adam and Eve. But Jesus Christ reversed the pattern and restored the possibility of the original relationship between God and humankind. When we try to function in the savior role in any form or fashion, it is harmful and debilitating to us and the person that we are attempting to save and rescue. Our efforts at saving people end tragically with people in worse shape than before we began.

I am convinced that most of us do not learn from insight. Edwin Friedman, following Murray Bowen, would say that nonmotivated people are impenetrable to insight.[2] This means that when people are not motivated to change, you can pour all the insight into them that you desire, and it will do no good. When people are unmotivated, giving them insight in the form of books, tapes, advice, counseling, prayer support, biblical teaching, preaching material, or any other form is useless. What motivates most of us to change is pain.

Most of us change when the pain of the old behavior becomes greater than the pain of making the new change. Most of us do not change until we are sick and tired of the pain. Once we are tired of hurting, then we are open to insight. Playing savior is the futile attempt to devise ways for people to change without feeling the pain and consequences of their behavior. It is attempting to take the pain away, which is to take the consequences away, and assuming that people will change because you have rescued them from the pain. When we take the pain away, we take away the prime motivation for change. When we take away the prime motivation for change, we run the dangerous risk that the person will become more dependent than ever before.

Rather than look at someone who played savior and attempted to take away the pain of another, let's look at someone who allowed another to experience the consequences of his behavior. Let's look at the healthy and mature responses of a father who assisted his son in deciding how he really wanted to live his life. Let's consider what I call the Parable of the Mature Father (Luke 15:11-27).

Most of us are familiar with this timeless story. A son came to his father and asked for his share of the father's estate. The father divided the estate and gave this son his portion. The son gathered all that he had and set off for a distant country. In the distant country, he squandered his inheritance in wild living. Just as he spent his last money, a famine arose in the land, and he was in need. He hired himself out to a citizen of that country who gave him the task of feeding the pigs. He was so hungry that he wanted to fill his stomach with some of the food that he was giving to the pigs. As he was experiencing the pain of the consequences of his actions, he came to himself. He decided that he would go home to his father and hire himself out as a servant there. He believed that even as a servant in his father's house he would receive better than he had in this distant country. The boy went home and asked his father for servant status. There was a reunion, and such was the joy of the father that he uttered the immortal words, "The son of mine who was dead is now alive; he that was lost is now found." The father killed the fatted calf and threw a restoration party.

I am most interested in the behavior of the father because the traditional interpretation of this story is that he intensely longed for his prodigal son and was filled with uncontrollable grief. I heard one preacher very aptly describe the father "sitting on the porch each day, tearfully and longingly looking up the road for the son to come home." This might be wonderful homiletic imagination and rhetorical flight, but it is not in the text. The text does not say anything about the father's posture while the son was gone.

I believe the father went on with his life. I believe the father assumed that the boy knew how to run his life and gave the boy the responsibility for it. I believe that when the father heard that the boy was in need, the father knew that to rescue his son would only hurt him in the long run. I believe the father allowed the boy to wallow in the pigpen; the father allowed the boy to experience the consequences of his behavior. The father went on with his life because he knew that we all have to feel the weight and gravity of our choices and decisions. He understood that if the son were going to mature, it would be because of the consequences of his choices. The father had the maturity to see that the pain and the lack of food could bring healing. The father believed that consequences heal.

Adam's response to the disobedience was to place blame and attempt to deny that he had done anything wrong. His attempt was to avoid the pain of the consequences. The pain of the consequences could heal, but Adam was not willing to go through that process. In contrast, the father allowed the son to go through the painful steps of his healing. The father allowed him to go through the famine, hard times, and the pigpen employment. As a result look at what the son says, "Father, I have sinned against heaven and you. I am no longer worthy to be called your son." Unlike Adam, there is no shifting of the blame; there is full responsibility for choices and actions.

I want to behave as a father towards my family, other people, and institutions. But often, I am tempted by the role of savior.

ANY STATEMENT THAT BEGINS WITH "HE/SHE/THEY CANNOT DO . . . FOR THEMSELVES" REFLECTS THE TEMPTATION TO PLAY SAVIOR.

Just as there was a litmus test for the role of victim, this is a litmus test for the role of savior. Anytime I catch myself thinking this thought or making this statement, I know that I am playing savior. Anytime that you do for others what they can and should do for themselves, you run the risk of playing savior.

As a pastor, I once talked with a daughter who was the sole caregiver for her elderly mother. She came in to see if I could help her find assistance from a church member because the burden of being sole caregiver was too great for her. After listening carefully, I pursued my sneaking suspicion that the mother was playing victim, and the daughter was playing savior. I asked her if she was taking away from her mother the opportunity to heal by assuming responsibility for many things that the mother could do for herself. Granted, because of her condition there were many things that she could not do, but after honest discussion the daughter admitted that there were many things that her mother could do. From that conversation I gleaned the truth of this principle: *Whenever you do for others what they can do for themselves, you run the risk of playing savior and leaving them more dependent.* We can help people and give the care that is much needed, but maybe help means never to do for people what they can do for themselves, especially if it risks leaving them more dependent.

Lesson 3:
The Dance of Immaturity—1 Kings 21

EVERY VICTIM NEEDS A SAVIOR, AND EVERY SAVIOR NEEDS A
VICTIM, AND VICTIM AND SAVIOR TOGETHER DO A DANCE OF
IMMATURITY THAT IS DESTRUCTIVE TO BOTH LIVES.

So Ahab went home, sullen and angry because Naboth the Jezreelite had said, "I will not give you the inheritance of my fathers." He lay on his bed sulking and refused to eat.

His wife Jezebel came in and asked him, "Why are you so sullen? Why won't you eat?"

He answered her, "Because I said to Naboth the Jezreelite, 'Sell me your vineyard; or if you prefer, I will give you another vineyard in its place.' But he said, 'I will not give you my vineyard.'"

Jezebel his wife said, "Is this how you act as king over Israel? Get up and eat! Cheer up. I'll get you the vineyard of Naboth the Jezreelite."

—1 Kings 21:4-7

We often discuss spiritual maturity without understanding that it is drastically affected by how much we play the roles of victim or savior. It is interesting that we often look at the person playing the role of victim as immature. It is more difficult for us to see that the person playing the role of savior has that same level of immaturity. We look at those in the role of savior as noble and heroic, and those in the role of victim as pathetic and weak. Until recently, it never dawned on me that while playing savior, I was equally immature, pathetic, and weak. When I could be honest about my own immaturity, I saw that playing the role of savior had to do with my own unresolved needs. I saw that I played savior in the lives of others to draw my attention away from my own pain. I found that playing savior and focusing on the inner life of others was prime avoidance of the pain of my own inner life. I was in no better shape than the victim. Victims erroneously believe that they are unable to do something, and saviors erroneously believe that they are able to do it for them or motivate them to do it. Every savior will find a victim, and every victim will find a savior. The savior and victim do a dance of immaturity that is destructive to both lives.

In Scripture, we find King Ahab and Queen Jezebel doing the dance of savior and victim (1 Kings 21). Ahab wanted Naboth's vineyard, but Naboth refused to sell it because his father had given him the land and therefore it was not for sale at any price. Ahab could not accept the fact that Naboth had the right to decide whether or not he wanted to sell the land. Ahab could not get his way, so he lay on the bed and played the role of victim.

His wife, Jezebel, came in and asked him why he was in this helpless condition. When Ahab told her it was because Naboth would not sell the land, she decided that Ahab was a wimp (he couldn't do it for himself), so she would get Naboth's vineyard for him. Jezebel should have recognized the right of Naboth not to sell his vineyard if he chose not to, and the right of her husband to respond more maturely to Naboth's choice, but she ignored all of that and played savior. She arranged for two scoundrels to testify that Naboth had cursed God and the king so that Naboth would be stoned for blasphemy and Ahab could take the land. Her plan succeeded, and Naboth was stoned to death. She said to Ahab, "Get up and take possession of the vineyard of Naboth. . . . He is no longer alive, but dead. " Ahab got up and took possession of the vineyard. Jezebel had rescued him, and now Ahab felt better.

Ahab had learned that the way to get what you want is to pretend to be helpless. Therefore, it was virtually guaranteed that Ahab would resort to more and more of this behavior. He would play the role of victim so well and so often that he would believe the role that he was playing. Jezebel would perceive herself to be more and more powerful as she continued to deliver what he needed. She would become a "superwoman."

Many women tell me that the role of superwoman is a frustrating, lonely, and exhausting one. A woman will eventually give up her life, hopes, and dreams, to continue to save her husband's life. He will descend into the role of "superwimp." He will become more and more helpless, more and more the victim. She will become more and more the savior. He will die of unused potential, and she will die of exhaustion.

Lesson 4:
Walk into the Storm—Matt. 14:22-33

ONE'S ABILITY TO ALLOW OTHERS TO EXPERIENCE PAIN AND CONSEQUENCES FOR THEMSELVES IS THE KEY TO AVOIDING THE POSTURE OF SAVIOR.

THE ABILITY TO TOLERATE AND HANDLE ONE'S OWN PAIN CONSTRUCTIVELY IS THE KEY TO AVOIDING THE POSTURE OF VICTIM.

During the fourth watch of the night Jesus went out to them, walking on the lake. When the disciples saw him walking on the lake, they were terrified. "It's a ghost," they said, and cried out in fear.

But Jesus immediately said to them: "Take courage! It is I. Don't be afraid."

"Lord, if it's you," Peter replied, "tell me to come to you on the water."

"Come," he said.

Then Peter got down out of the boat, walked on the water and came toward Jesus. But when he saw the wind, he was afraid and, beginning to sink, cried out, "Lord, save me!"

Immediately Jesus reached out his hand and caught him. "You of little faith," he said, "why did you doubt?"

—Matt. 14:25-31

The roles of victim and savior are both defeated strategies that we implement in the midst of the pain of life in an attempt to feel better. Life seems easier if we believe that someone has done us in (victim), or if we can ignore our own issues and rescue others from their pain (savior). Life seems better if we are able to blame them for our misery and pain, or if we can see ourselves as rescuers from pain and, therefore, as heroic and noble. Rather than face the fact that psychic pain is an inevitable breach between what we expect to get and what we actually receive, we find someone to blame or save so we can feel better. Rather than do the work of maturity and adjust our expectations to what we can reasonably accomplish within the limits of being human, we play the role of savior or victim. Many of us refuse to accept the fact that pain communicates the need for an adjustment in expectations. Pain is what God uses to move us from victims or saviors to human beings who accept the finite limits of our time, knowledge, and power.

When I look deeply at my psychic pain, I find that it is based in my lack of acceptance of the natural limits of life. What it means to be a human being is that there are natural limits to our time, knowledge, and power. For example, there are natural limits to our power: we cannot change anyone or make anyone do or become anything based on our own needs, wants, desires, or expectations. In truth, the only person that we can change is ourselves, and changing ourselves is a Herculean task.

I have experienced a tremendous amount of pain attempting to change others. I spend far too much energy attempting to make others become what I want them to be. Sometimes it is subtle through manipulation; other times it is overt by telling them "the truth that they really need to hear." When I reach beyond my limits and attempt to change people, the result is basically the same: pain and injury. When I attempt to play God (savior), then the result is pain in the relationship between that person and me—the result of expectations that are beyond the limits of being human. My pain lessens when I am able to accept that the other person is free to choose what is in his or her best interest, and my best choice is to accept that decision and live with it. My pain lessens when I accept the limitations of my power—the reality that I am only human.

If we can accept and face the pain, learn from it, and accept the limits of life that it teaches, then we will grow and mature. If we constructively handle our pain, we will develop reasonable expectations of life that remove the apparent necessity of playing the role of victim or savior. A metaphor that helps and reminds me to handle the pain of life constructively is walking into a storm. Playing the role of victim or savior is avoiding the storm. If we are interested in spiritual growth and maturity, then we must learn to walk into the storm. We must face the fear, uncertainty, doubt, and pain in order to gain maturity.

In Matthew 14, Peter walked right into the storm. As the wind and waves buffeted the disciples' boat, Jesus spoke to calm them saying,

"It is I. Do not be afraid." Peter got out of the boat and walked on the water toward Jesus. He walked into the storm. But when Peter began to sink, he cried out "Lord, save me." Jesus reached out his hand, caught him and said, "You of little faith, why did you doubt?" One of the comforts of trusting in Jesus Christ is that we will never sink. We might go down in the water, but we will never sink and drown. The Lord will be with us to guide and rescue us. With Jesus you will get to the other side. The fact that Jesus was there to help Peter gives us courage to walk into the storm because we have an encourager, a comforter, and a rescuer who will help us get to the other side. We are not alone. I believe at the center of much of the pain of our lives, God is inviting us to walk into the storm to meet God.

The key to staying out of the position of victim is to walk into the storms in our lives. The key to staying out of the position of savior is to allow others to have the opportunity to walk into the storms in their lives. Victim and savior are roles that we play to avoid walking into the storms of life. We must let the victim and savior roles go and walk into the depths of the pain of life, knowing that we are never alone.

THE MATURE CHURCH MEMBER

After making the decision to live a Victorious Christian Life and gauging our personal maturity, we must negotiate a healthy relationship with a body of believers. How does personal maturity look when it is expressed in the congregational body? How does maturity look and behave in the corporate church setting? The principles discussed in this module minimize unhealthy conflict and emphasize the personal and spiritual maturity that contributes to corporate maturity.

Lesson 1:
The Privilege of Participation—John 15:12-15

THE MOST SIGNIFICANT OPPORTUNITY AND BENEFIT A
CONGREGATION GIVES TO A MEMBER IS THE PRIVILEGE OF
PARTICIPATION, WHICH IS THE RESPONSIBILITY AND RIGHT
TO CONTRIBUTE TO THE WORK OF THE CONGREGATION.

> *"My command is this: Love each other as I have loved you. Greater love has no one than this, that he lay down his life for his friends. You are my friends if you do what I command. I no longer call you servants, because a servant does not know his master's business. Instead, I have called you friends, for everything that I learned from my Father I have made known to you."*
>
> *—John 15:12-15*

In the Farewell Discourses of John 14–17, Jesus gives the command to the disciples that they love one another as he has loved them. He illustrates his great love for them by telling them that persons can give no greater love than laying down their lives for their friends. The disciples are not able to understand the full meaning of his words because they do not yet understand that he will lay down his life for them.

27

Through the experience of Calvary, they will come to understand the true nature of Jesus' sacrificial love. He tells them that he no longer considers them servants because everything God has made known to him, he has made known to them. Jesus has told them everything that God has told him because he considers them friends.

I interpret the term *friends* to mean more than what we commonly think of in relational terms, such as *pals* or *buddies*. *Friends* is a functional term that describes an important component of the relationship Jesus had with the disciples; I prefer to interpret "friends" to mean "equals." Jesus valued the disciples as equals and did not withhold information from them but relayed to them everything he had received from God. Jesus bestowed upon the disciples the privilege of participation.

The privilege of participation is the gift that we give when we decide to treat each other equally rather than subserviently or unequally. Unequal relationships usually take the form of master-servant, or dominant-subordinate. Unequal relationships mitigate against the privilege of participation because the climate is one of control and coercion through the selective dissemination of information. The result of the selective, false information, or what could be called propaganda, is that the dominators police and control their subordinates in order to maintain rule, and the subordinates feign immaturity to force the dominators to be responsible for them. Where there is selective information, dominators force subordinates to be subordinate, and subordinates force dominators to dominate. Both subordinates and dominators believe the selective, false information, and this belief establishes and reinforces the unhealthy climate surrounding a relationship in which neither subordinates nor dominators have the privilege of participation. But where there is truth, there is equality and the privilege of participation.

I do not want to give the illusion that equality implies that there is no rank or hierarchy such as is proposed in an egalitarian society. There is hierarchy in all living things, but when equality is one of the basic beliefs of hierarchy, then hierarchy becomes functional rather than restrictive. Functional hierarchy allows the dissemination of true and timely information in order to link "diverse levels of responsibility and contribution among members" rather than to enforce dominant-subordinate relationships.[1] In functional hierarchy, information links us in order to accomplish tasks rather than to determine our rank or our importance. Functional hierarchy works in ways that combine the best features of hierarchy—stability, order, and harmony—with the best features of egalitarian society—cooperation and mutual benefits.[2]

The purpose of functional hierarchy is to give people true and timely information so they can make the critical decisions of their lives. Information is the raw material from which people construct their understanding of their situation and define their options.[3] In dominant-subordinate relationships, understandings of reality and options are defined by dominators. Fundamentally, the privilege of participation is the commitment to give true and timely information so that people can construct their reality and shape their options.

It has taken me many years to experience and learn the truth concerning the privilege of participation. At my former church, New Faith Baptist Church, I often unintentionally functioned opposite the principle of the privilege of participation. I functioned based on what I have come to call "overfunctioning" and "the cult of personality." To fully understand my flawed functioning, we must take a systematic look at overfunctioning and the cult of personality.

Personal Dimensions of Overfunctioning

Overfunctioning is a dysfunctional character trait in the leader. The leader attempts to relieve the spiritual, physical, and emotional distress of others, no matter the cost to the leader's person and family. The following, a confessional statement that I wrote at the end of my ministry at the New Faith Baptist Church, demonstrates the devastating effects of overfunctioning:

I feel responsible for the spiritual, physical, and emotional well-being of the entire congregation. This leads me to feel required by others, and requiring of myself more than can be realistically accomplished by one human being. This leads to a style that is oriented to pleasing—an attempt to be accepted by all—and the attitude of relieving the spiritual, emotional, and physical distress of others at all costs. This leads to feeling overloaded, overwhelmed, overworked, and undersupported in ministry. While I overfunction at work, I totally underfunction at home with my wife, family, and kids. And in following the overfunctioning pattern to its logical conclusion, I completely neglect my own spiritual, physical, and emotional health. I must make new choices, or make an early exit from the ministry or this world as a superhuman fool.

Overfunctioning is the neurotic condition of perceiving oneself as stuck with the entire responsibility for an organization or family, and the anxious determination to fulfill all requirements of the perception no matter the costs. It is the foolish attempt to do excessively more than one's fair share.

Organizational Dimensions of Overfunctioning

As a result of structural defects in the spiritual, physical, and emotional makeup of some organizations, overfunctioning is the standard expectation for leadership. In those organizations, the corporate ethos requires leaders to overfunction. Reflecting on that organizational pattern, a colleague and I wrote the following statement:

> I have noticed that many fellow pastors and some congregational members are not only openly suspicious of the movement toward shared vision, leadership, and responsibility, but are often highly resistant. Historically, the role of the pastor/leader in racial ethnic groups like Koreans and African Americans, has primacy given to strict, solo leadership. There has been an often unspoken expectation that leaders have God-given, unquestionable authority and responsibility. With this as the overarching paradigm, can partnership and shared leadership work in the African American church? Or, is overfunctioning the destiny of those who lead in the African American context? Is this a paradigm in the African American community that goes beyond the black church to African American businesses and schools? Do we dare suggest that at least one critical factor in the reality that many African American institutions have such a hard time perpetuating themselves from generation to generation is overfunctioning leadership and the overfunctioning expectation for leadership?[4]

The organization desires that the leader take spiritual, physical, and emotional responsibility for its well-being. The organization places itself in the subordinate role, or what could be called underfunctioning, and forces the leader to be dominant. Overfunctioning is a flaw in the person of the leader joined with an underfunctioning weakness in the structure of the organization. Overfunctioning and underfunctioning create a partnership between a flawed leader and a flawed organization. This partnership has devastating consequences for both.

The Cult of Personality

The cult of personality is closely related to overfunctioning and underfunctioning because it makes those behaviors necessary. The pastor, operating from within the framework of the cult of personality, is afforded strict, solo leadership with unquestionable authority and responsibility. Because all authority and responsibility is held by the leader, the success or failure of the organization is attributed to the leader. Invariably, in this framework the pastor overfunctions and the congregation underfunctions.

The cult of personality is operative when a key individual or individuals shoulder the unquestioned authority and responsibility for the well-being of the organization or family, and everyone works to support this person in upholding the weight of the group. The family or organization responds to the agenda of this one person or one group of people. Often there are boards and committees, but none of them set the agenda—they respond to the agenda set by the personality. Boards, councils, or committees can be in the position of sanctioning or not sanctioning the agenda of the personality or personalities, but they have no independent agenda of their own to act on.

Many might ask, "But what is wrong with this kind of functioning? There are many effective models of church and organizational life that have followed this model and done extremely well." I agree that many have done well with this model, but I would respond, "At what cost to the leader and the leader's family, and at what cost to the church family?" The problem with the cult of personality is that it overuses and burns out the leader, and it fails to develop the rest of the people who could participate more. Over time, the one who overfunctions often becomes angry, hurt, and bitter about congregational dependency and the tremendous weight and load of ministry. At the same time, the underfunctioning ones are angry, hurt, and bitter because of their dependency and the fact that they do not get the chance to make a full contribution or have the privilege to participate as equals. The cult of personality leads to anger and frustration on both sides that will sooner or later erupt with devastating consequences. Sometimes it explodes in the spiritual, physical, and emotional health of the leader, in the health of the leader's family, in the health of others in the congregation, or in congregational health itself, creating conflicts, such as power plays, church fights, splits, and court fights.

The cult of personality also has a difficult time with succession. How will personality-driven leadership replace or duplicate itself? The system must find another personality-driven leader who must copy the leadership style of the predecessor. After one or two generations, it gets difficult to continue to find the same type of personality driven leaders. Sooner or later, an organization that wants to survive in the long term must move beyond the cult of personality.

I do not want to suggest that the cult of personality is evil—it is the first phase of the life for most organizations. It is only when we cannot move to the second phase—where personality is balanced by process and fact—that it becomes ultimately destructive. The cult of personality is the first phase of organizational life in much the way that we are dependent on our parents and family for our existence in the first phase of our lives. But just as it is destructive to the human personality to remain in the stage of dependency, so it is destructive for organizations and families to remain in the first phase. I believe that the goal of the second phase of organizational life is for personality to be balanced by processes and facts. We cannot deny that personality will always be a critical part of leadership, but we seek to *balance* personality with processes and facts. This balance moves the organization into the functional hierarchy of equality and the privilege of participation.

As an example of personality balanced by process and fact, consider a mother and father struggling together to open a small bakery. Mom and Dad put in untold hours in the first phase of the life of the business, and it is successful while being personality driven. By the sheer force of will and determination in the personalities of Mom and Dad, the business moves forward and expands to its second and third location. Mom and Dad raise the oldest son in the business and secretly hope that he will succeed them in its ownership. They send him to get a master's degree in business so he will come back home and work under them to solidify and transition the business.

The son comes home, and the first thing that he does is establish a voucher system for checks. No one can get a check without filling out a voucher with supporting documentation. The dad comes in for a check and refuses to fill out the paper work. He says to the son, "I am not going to fill out a voucher. I built this business from nothing." The dad must realize that it is true that he built the business, but if it is going to survive beyond him, then he will need to put systems and processes in place that allow the business to run based on something in addition to personality. These processes and systems will balance the personality and allow the business to move forward no matter who is the leader. If the dad allows the son the privilege of participation, then the organization can move beyond the cult of personality. If the dad does not allow the son the privilege of participation, the business, in all likelihood, will never go beyond the level of what Mom and Dad could accomplish.

This is very much true in the church as well. The pastor that has, by sheer force of will and determination, helped the church to prosper must fill out a voucher with supporting documentation if the church is to go to the next level. The central personality must allow for fact-based systems and processes that will counterbalance the personality and allow the organization a future beyond the present leadership.

The privilege of participation is agreeing that we will not function based on the cult of personality. It is the spiritual commitment to the standard of equality for each member of the Body. We will not require one person to overfunction while most of us underfunction. We will grace each other with the status of equals and extend to each other the privilege to participate. We all need to be able to give each other the gift of letting information flow such that we all can make the best choices for our lives. The church hierarchy functions to disseminate information so that as many members as possible have the awesome privilege to participate, the privilege to make a meaningful contribution, the privilege to find fellowship and equal relationship, the privilege to have their gifts affirmed and respected, and the privilege to grow and develop by gaining new skills and experiences. The church is the clearinghouse through which the privileges flow. I believe that Jesus meant this and intended this when he called the disciples *friends*.

Lesson 2:
Love and the Privilege of Participation—
1 Cor. 12:31b-13:3

THE ULTIMATE VALUE OF MEMBERS AND LEADERS TO THE
CONGREGATION IS NOT JUDGED BY THE ORTHODOXY OF THEIR
BELIEFS, THE SIZE OF THEIR CONTRIBUTIONS, OR THE LENGTH
OF THEIR SERVICE, BUT BY HOW WELL THEY UPHOLD THE
PRINCIPLE OF THE PRIVILEGE OF PARTICIPATION.

And now I will show you the most excellent way.
If I speak in the tongues of men and of angels, but have not
love, I am only a resounding gong or a clanging cymbal. If I
have the gift of prophecy and can fathom all mysteries and all
knowledge, and if I have a faith that can move mountains, but
have not love, I am nothing. If I give all I possess to the poor
and surrender my body to the flames, but have not love, I gain
nothing.
                                      —1 Cor. 12:31b–13:3

The Corinthian church had an equality problem that Paul addressed in his first letter to them. Some in the church had set themselves up as superior to the rest of the believers in the Body. Paul believed that there was little else more harmful to the church than superiority and arrogance on the part of believers, especially toward one another. In 1 Cor. 3:1-9, Paul mentions a division in the Body because some claimed to be superior as followers of Apollos, and others, as followers of Paul. In 4:6-7, some set themselves up as superior because of their biblical knowledge and their ability to add secular wisdom to the written word of God. Some had become so full of spiritual pride that Paul accused them of being downright arrogant (4:18). Some even challenged his apostolic authority and ability (9:1-4). In chapters 12–14, some people positioned themselves as more spiritual because they felt that they had been given supernatural gifts. The in the Body who had those gifts—speaking in tongues, healing, or prophesying—considered themselves more spiritual than those who had the gift of administration.

Paul corrected the arrogance in the Corinthian church by reminding its members that maturity was the issue, not gifts. Through the same Spirit, God gives gifts to everyone, but God does not give everyone the same gift. All gifts are equal and needed if the church is going to accomplish its work, and, therefore, no one can boast or claim to be better than another.

Paul used the imagery of the human body because it is one entity that has many parts. The church is one Body that has many parts, and no one part is superior to another part. All parts are needed, and therefore equal. The sign of maturity is not that one is gifted but that with one's gift one can function equally and in harmony with others' gifts. Paul believed that maturity is building other people up with one's gift.

If Paul was right, then spiritual maturity is not necessarily dependent on gifts, human wisdom, or any human attribute because all of these tend to puff people up. Spiritual maturity is based on love, which builds people up. Spiritual maturity is allowing love to regulate one's gift to build other people up and is, therefore, the most excellent way. Paul attempts to show this to the Corinthian church in 12:31b—13:3:

> And now I will show you the most excellent way. If I speak in the tongues of men and angels, but have not love, I am only a resounding gong or a clanging cymbal. If I have the gift of prophecy and can fathom all mysteries and all knowledge, and if I have a faith that can move mountains, but have not love, I am nothing. If I give all I possess to the poor and surrender my body to the flames, but have not love, I gain nothing.

If I exercise my gift, but it does not build anyone up, then I am nothing but a noisy gong and a clanging cymbal. Equality is one of the cardinal principles of love, which extends to others the privilege of participation.

Maturity based on love rather than knowledge is a radical and revolutionary concept for most of us. The term *knowledge* is representative of all the human efforts we make in a competitive world to establish, justify, and make ourselves better than others around us. Usually, we base maturity on knowledge, human effort, ingenuity, or accomplishments. Sometimes knowledge is just an exaltation of ourselves based on what we know about the Scriptures or secular human wisdom. Other times we laud orthodoxy of belief: a person must have right belief, and if a person has right belief, then he or she is spiritually superior. Other times we value the size of people's financial contributions to the church or how long they or their families have been in service to the church. We use these kinds of markers to establish the "spiritual ones."

Following Paul, I believe that the spiritual ones are those who exercise their gifts with love. The spiritual ones are those who use their gifts to build up other people rather than themselves. A person's value to the body is determined in direct proportion to how he or she holds to the ethic of love in building up other people by extending to them the privilege of participation. The mature member is the one who can adhere to a standard of true, reliable, and timely information and who allows people the opportunity to rightly discern their options and choose their best interests. I understand now why there is such a close connection between truth and love. Love is providing true information that allows me to choose what is best for my life. The concept of the privilege of participation is the true basis of judgment as to the value and worth of a member.

It is easy to abuse the privilege of participation because many of us have been denied love, truth, and equality, which are rare in human relationships. Many of the relationships that we are involved in have adopted dominant-subordinate tendencies. If we think about the relationships that are the most profitable and valuable to us, they are the ones in which we are treated as equals, whereas some of our most devastating relationships occur when the people we love do not treat us as equals. Because equality is such a rare phenomenon in our relationships, it is very easy for some to abuse the privilege of participation.

In the next several lessons, I teach the privilege of participation and talk about abuses of it so that we can examine ourselves and make necessary adjustments.

Lesson 3: Abuse by Secrets

THE MOST GRIEVOUS ABUSE OF THE PRIVILEGE OF PARTICIPATION IS TRAFFICKING IN SECRETS, THAT IS, RUMORS, GOSSIP, INFORMATION LEAKS, THIRD-PARTY INFORMATION, ANONYMOUS LETTERS, AND CHURCH INTELLIGENCE AND ESPIONAGE.

Information is the key to equality. True and timely information guarantees that people have the opportunity to define their options and make the best choices for their lives. In many organizations and families, information is not handled adequately or appropriately. For example, in an organization that is operating out of the dominant-subordinate model, the dominators have the information and selectively share it with the subordinates. The subordinates need to know what can affect their lives so they resort to leaks, rumors, second-hand information, and gossip in an attempt to stay informed. The dominators realize that there is information leakage and become even stingier and more closed-mouthed with information. This forces the subordinates to go to even greater measures of intelligence and espionage, and this leads the dominators to take yet greater measures of security and concealment. The games go on and on, and both are caught in a vicious circle of hide-and-seek. The sum total of this is handling information in ways that abuse equality and the privilege of participation on both sides.

In this atmosphere of hide-and-seek, it is very difficult for information to be presented as true and timely because of the concealment, leaks, rumors, and gossip that saturate the environment. People are not able to define their options and make the best choices because the privilege of participation has been abused. I have been a pastor for more than twenty years, and I have seen a tremendous amount of erratic behavior in churches and within myself. When we get right down to it, we can only act within the purview of the information that we have. It would not be an exaggeration to say that one's impressions, feelings, thoughts, behavior, and theorizing are all based on the information one has obtained. To the extent that the information is not correct, all of these things could be wrong.

I make an attempt to view much of the erratic behavior in churches and organizations as a lack of information: "Distressful behavior is often the consequence of deprivation of information in a person, family, organization, community, or government. Without access to information, we tend to fill in the gaps with our fantasies, our projections, and our past experiences (all of which can lead to dysfunctional behavior."[5] This helps me to view much of the "drama" that is so much a part of church and family life as a deprivation of information. When people do not have, or do not trust that they have, reliable information, they fill in the perceived gaps with (1) trafficking in gossip, rumors, and third party information or (2) personal projections, fantasies, and past negative experiences. I sum up the deprivation of information by using the term *secrets*. Secrets are devastating to the privilege of participation because they color and distort the flow of information. Secrets are the abuse of the privilege of participation.

I believe that there are primarily three kinds of secrets that operate in any church or family life: (1) the "I will tell you, but do not tell anyone else" secret, (2) the nobody talks about it secret, and (3) the scattered opinions and unsubstantiated perceptions secret.

"I Will Tell You, but Do Not Tell Anyone Else"

Family member A gives information to family member B and asks family member B not to tell family members C through Z. A and B process subsequent family information differently from C through Z because A and B know the secret. This creates a problem since C through Z lack the information that A and B have. A church example is similar: elder A tells elder B that the senior pastor is having an affair and asks elder B not to tell elders C through Z. A meeting is held to consider a raise for the senior pastor, and elders A and B vote "no" when everyone else unanimously votes yes. The rest of the group cannot understand why A and B are dissenting. In another example, a teenager tells her dad that she is having sex and begs him not to tell Mom. Mom allows the teenager to stay out late with her boyfriend. Dad hears about it and explodes at Mom's "lack of parenting skills."

We make critical decisions based on the information that we are able to gather. People who do not have all the information are at a distinct disadvantage in decision making.

Nobody Talks about It

Bad situations occur in family life, but sometimes there is an understanding that nobody should ever talk about them. Families have subjects or people that are unmentionable, and everyone in the family knows it. The same is true in the church. For example, a long-time member and chairperson of the finance committee embezzles $2,000 of church funds, resigns, and leaves town when caught. For fear of reprisal by the members, the church leaders do not inform the membership of the facts. The leaders decide never to mention the member or the incident. Everyone knows that something tragic happened because a long-time member is gone, but no one can talk about it because the leaders have agreed to keep it a secret. Of course it *is* talked about; the grapevine has it that he disappeared because he embezzled church funds, but nobody will ever talk about it in the open. The church has played the "nobody talks about it, but everybody knows" game.

In the family, a young man dies of AIDS-related complications, and no one ever talks about it because of embarrassment. In the open, the cause of death soon becomes a great mystery, though everyone knows in private that he died of AIDS-related complications. It is amazing how many families play the "nobody knows but everybody knows" game.

Scattered Opinions and Unsubstantiated Perceptions

Opinions and perceptions are often accepted at face value and not checked out. People believe and act on all kinds of rumors, lies, and gossip because there is no filter or screen for adding or subtracting legitimacy from idle conversation and gossip. In this environment, the worst is believed about people without any benefit of the doubt.

We are responsible for confirming our opinions and values relative to the facts. For example, a rumor starts in the church that money is missing and church funds have been misappropriated. An angry group of members shows up at the congregational meeting demanding resignations and firings. They submit a petition demanding the resignation of the senior pastor, and they accuse anyone who requests an investigation into the facts of covering up for the pastor. In the family, an aunt will not allow her niece to spend the night because she does not want the niece to associate with her daughter. The family grapevine has it that the niece is known to be sexually active and has had two abortions. Despite the daughter's tearful pleas, her mother will not allow the niece to come over and will not allow the daughter to go over to the niece's home. As parents, we have the right to carefully attend to the company our children keep, but we must do so based on the facts, and not the family grapevine.

Secrets about other people are devastating to family and congregational life because of what they do to perceptions—they cause people to form perceptions that people mistake as reality. These kinds of secrets maintain perceptions through illusions, preventing the admission of contradictory evidence. Often, we filter out information that does not fit with our secrets. This filtered-out information could, in a more open and non-hide-and-seek environment, change the perception, but secrets fix perceptions and make them beliefs.

Secrets about other people create false bonds and unnecessary estrangements. Once I tell you a secret about someone else and swear you to secrecy, we have a bond. It is a false bond because true bonds cannot be built on secrets about someone else. True relationships with people are built on confidential and secret information that I share about myself and that the other person shares with me about him- or herself.

Church leaders should commit to abandoning the hide-and-seek game of concealment by giving the membership true and timely information that allows them to shape their options and make the best decisions about what is in the church's interest. Church members should commit to abandoning the hide-and-seek game of intelligence and espionage through leaks and rumors by respecting confidentiality and trusting in the leaders' ability to provide true and timely information.

I do not want to imply that the privilege of participation means that we are totally egalitarian with information—that everyone, in other words, has the right to know all information at all times. I believe that information must flow through some kind of hierarchy. This natural flow means that some will have information before others because of their functional position as leaders. Confidentiality is the art of holding information until the best and appropriate time for people to know. For example, if a company were going to merge and close, it would not be appropriate for the CEO to share that information before the deal has been finalized. For the good of everyone, the information has to be held in confidence until the appropriate time to share it.

Secrets occur when we go beyond the point where people should be given information, but still have not. They occur when we keep in confidence facts that should be open information. An example of a secret would be if the church were behind in the budget to the extent that everyone had to be laid off except the pastor, and the true financial reality were only made public six months after the people had been laid off. The word *timely,* as a descriptor in the definition of the privilege of participation, means that there is an appropriate time for information to be shared. Out of the privilege of participation, I have made this commitment to my congregation and church staff, "I will share with you as much information as I can, as soon as I can."

Lesson 4:
Abuse by Scapegoating—John 11:49-53

THE DIRECT OPPOSITE OF THE PRIVILEGE OF PARTICIPATION
IS RESOLVING CHURCH AND FAMILY CONFLICTS THROUGH
SCAPEGOATING.

*Then one of them, named Caiaphas, who was high priest that
year, spoke up, . . . "You do not realize that it is better for you
that one man die for the people than that the whole nation
perish."*
—John 11:49-50

Sometimes we learn to clarify a truth by considering its stark and naked opposite. I would like to do this with the privilege of participation using
its absolute opposite, which is scapegoating. The opposite of partic-
ipating as an equal is being excluded and demonized.

Walter Wink, in his famous book *Engaging the Powers: Discernment and Resistance in a World of Domination,* helped me to do critical thinking about the management of conflict through the
methodology of scapegoating in families.[6] After reflecting on Wink's
work, I believe that too often in family and congregational life, we
scapegoat people and groups.

It is the relational pattern of human beings to fall headlong into
ever-escalating cycles of conflict and violent retaliation, which can
create large-scale adversarial relationships like those of Serbs and Al-
banians, Jews and Palestinians, Hutus and Tutsis, and Irish Catholics
and Irish Protestants. While not everyone in the entire human family
is involved in such a conflict, human history shows that people can
fight for generations with escalating cycles of violence and hatred.

Even as we participate in this destructive behavior, we realize that
this pattern cannot continue infinitely because at some point the entire human race would be in danger of extinction. To stop the retaliation cycle, both groups find a scapegoat—someone on whom they
can perform a symbolic final killing. In other words, to stop killing
each other both groups find someone they can agree to kill to resolve
their violence and anger toward each other. The violence is discharged onto the scapegoat, and the human race is protected from
extinction.

Traditionally, the scapegoat is taken to the edge of a cliff. The entire community forms a half-circle and throws stones at it. Because everyone throws stones, everyone is guilty, and no one is guilty. With violence discharged onto the scapegoat, the group can now redirect its energies toward mutual cooperation and even reconciliation.

In modern times, we do not literally send the scapegoat into the desert or stone the scapegoat, but we do blame and target people who are outsiders, different, or are "sinners." I have seen families scapegoat an alcoholic relative, a teen-age unwed mother, and gay or lesbian family members who become the source of family embarrassment or other problems. The family calms itself down by casting its blame, sin, and conflict onto one person. On a larger scale, Northern Republicans and Southern Democrats settled their differences with the Compromise of 1877, which officially ended Reconstruction, abandoned Freedman's rights, and inaugurated an era of lynchings and terrorism against blacks. On the international scale, the Israeli-Palestinian conflict is an example of how retaliatory violence can escalate to extreme levels as people scapegoat each other. While most situations do not escalate to this extent, small-scale violence and cycles of blame and mistrust are very common.

As Wink points out, the scapegoat is generally someone who is either disabled, marginal, a foreigner, a newcomer, an eccentric, a communist, a witch, a homosexual, a purveyor of new ideas, or a prophet. *A scapegoat has to be someone whose death or expulsion no one will avenge.* The cycle of violence is broken because the perception is that there is no one to retaliate.[7]

The truth, of course, is that someone *will* avenge every scapegoat's death. Usually, no matter how marginal or outcast the scapegoat may appear, someone emerges from somewhere to take up the scapegoat's cause. This means that sooner or later the groups are back to their escalating cycles of retaliation. Though it first appeared that there was peace and reconciliation, suddenly the retaliatory cycle is operative again. The cycle continues until the groups can find the next scapegoat.

I believe that the church of Jesus Christ has functioned in the scapegoat model much too often. Conflict in churches has been resolved by the inappropriate banishment, firing, dismissal, ostracizing, censoring, excommunication, and alienation of persons or groups that all agree are the troublemakers. We have sometimes randomly selected the one that we believe no one will avenge in order to attempt to resolve our conflict and maintain peace in the household of faith. We must discern whether this is consistent with the gospel. Is scapegoating a model of conflict resolution that God would approve of? What does the Bible have to say about scapegoating? What would be a way of living together and working through our conflict that does not involve scapegoating?

Wink teaches that the Bible radically departs from the human system of scapegoating and cycles of retaliation even though the violence of the Old Testament is plain to all. Wink quotes Raymond Schwager, who points out that in the Old Testament there are six hundred passages of explicit violence, one thousand passages where God's own violent actions of punishment are described, one hundred passages where God expressly commands others to kill people, and several stories where God tries to kill for no apparent reason (e.g., Exod. 4:24-26).[8] Violence is one of the central activities and major themes of the Old Testament.

Wink acknowledges that violence, but points out that the Old Testament records God standing on the side of the victim for the first time in human history: God is identified with scapegoats and victims of violence. Wink points to the Exodus and the suffering servant texts of Isaiah as prime examples of God's becoming involved in a scapegoat's suffering. God is on the side of the liberation and vindication of scapegoats. Wink quotes René Girard, who understands the Old Testament as a "long and laborious exodus out of the world of violence and sacred projections, an exodus plagued by many reversals and falling short of its goal."[9] The Old Testament participates in the very painful march to a new order of human behavior that does not use violence to resolve human conflict and does not project human violence onto God.

In the New Testament, God fully identifies with the victims of scapegoating. Girard points out that the New Testament is a collection of books written from the point of view of victims and scapegoats. Jesus is victim and scapegoat, and the Gospels go to great lengths to demonstrate that he is innocent of being the enemy of the state and religion.[10] The writer of the Gospel of John reports that Caiaphas, the high priest, says to the Sanhedrin that it is better that Jesus die than for the whole nation to perish. It is clear that Jesus' enemies plot his death so that he can serve as a scapegoat.

Jesus voluntarily and willingly becomes the scapegoat to unmask and overcome the scapegoat system. In Jesus, God does not demand sacrifices—God becomes the sacrifice. God puts an end once and for all to the sacrificial system of scapegoating. The resurrection is the guarantee that the human order of scapegoating is replaced by a new ethic. In John 11:51-52, Caiaphas prophesied beyond himself that Jesus' death would bring together the "scattered children of God, . . . and make them one." The Gospels announce and authenticate a new human order of behavior: the resolution of differences according to the ethics and standards of the kingdom of God. Love is the new ethic of conflict resolution.

The death and resurrection of Jesus mean that God does not endorse holy wars or religious violence or the violent seizure of the kingdom of God. God does not endorse violence with a religious base and a spiritual justification. If this were the case, Jesus would have used violence to overcome evil. He did not call down legions of angels, but endured death on the cross. Jesus calls for a different way of confronting evil. Jesus demonstrates that it is impossible to overcome evil with evil because as soon as you do that, the spirit of the enemy has already defeated you. And despite your seeming victory over evil, the actual defeat is in the fact that you have become evil. Jesus teaches that you cannot murder because as soon as you murder, you become a murderer. You cannot secure peace through violence. Jesus overcomes evil with good.

I want to be careful here to plainly state that I do not mean that evil is not to be confronted, resisted, and fought. I am raising the concern of the *means* one chooses to overcome evil. If one chooses the means of evil to attempt to overcome evil, then one becomes evil. This is why the New Testament says, "The weapons of our warfare are not carnal, but are good for the pulling down of strongholds" (2 Cor. 10:4-5). This text tells us that God requires the unconditional and unilateral renunciation of violence as a method of advancing the kingdom. Love is the spiritual weapon that pulls down evil strongholds.

Lesson 5:
The Illusion of Participation—Matt. 5:33-37

THE WITHDRAWAL OF FINANCIAL, SPIRITUAL, OR PHYSICAL PARTICIPATION AND SUPPORT, BUT NOT MEMBERSHIP, TO PROTEST A PASTORAL, LEADERSHIP, OR CONGREGATIONAL DECISION IS AN ABUSE OF THE PRIVILEGE OF PARTICIPATION.

*"Again, you have heard that it was said to the people long ago,
'Do not break your oath, but keep the oaths you have made to
the Lord.' But I tell you, Do not swear at all: either by heaven,
for it is God's throne; or by the earth, for it is his footstool; or by
Jerusalem, for it is the city of the Great King. And do not swear
by your head, for you cannot make even one hair white or
black. Simply let your 'Yes' be 'Yes,' and your 'No,' 'No'; anything beyond this comes from the evil one."*

—*Matt. 5:33-37*

In this text, Jesus gives instruction against the practice of making oaths.
Mosaic Law allowed the Lord's name to be invoked, which meant any
vow to which it was attached became a vow to the Lord. However, the
Law forbade irreverent oaths, light use of the Lord's name, and broken vows. Making oaths became very complicated, with much rab-
binic discussion judging how binding an oath was by examining how
closely it related to Yahweh's name. For example, swearing by heaven
and earth was not binding, though swearing by Jerusalem was. The
main point of the original teaching of the Old Testament was the
fundamental importance of complete and constant truthfulness, and
God's name was the guarantee of one's truthfulness.

Jesus breaks through these layers of interpretation and returns to
the original Old Testament meaning, minus God's name as a guarantee. For Jesus, if one does not swear at all, then one cannot possibly swear falsely. Jesus says in verse 37, "Let your 'Yes' be 'Yes' and
your 'No,' 'No.'" He is suggesting that we be consistently truthful, that
we do not use vows to threaten or evade the truth, that we do not use
God's name or swearing to guarantee our truth. Jesus is saying,
plainly and simply, "Tell the truth." He expects a believer to tell truth
so consistently that the believer is known for telling the truth and the
believer's own word has its own legitimacy. Jesus expects the believer
to be clear and decisive so that people can count on his or her word.
If we are going to exercise the privilege of participation, let us exercise the privilege or participation. Let us not give the illusion of participation. Let your "Yes" be "Yes" and your "No" be "No."

The privilege of participation is a great benefit of inclusion, but
we must guard against the illusion of participation, which can be giving in to the temptation to withdraw our financial, spiritual, or physical support from our congregation to protest a direction or decision
by a leader or the leadership. Sometimes we are so strongly against a

decision that we are compelled to withdraw our membership. (I will discuss that in the next lesson.) But the illusion of participation is withdrawing without leaving and quitting while pretending that we are still on the team. It is turning our backs on the essentials of participation while feigning mature church membership.

Usually when the subject of morale comes up in discussion, I hear people gauging where they are in regard to the privilege of participation. Often when people say, "Morale is low in the church," or even that their own morale is low, I hear the illusion of participation. I hear the withdrawal of physical or spiritual support. Often when there is low morale there is the withdrawal of cheerfulness, confidence, and willingness to perform. When this occurs, the one with the low morale often attempts to shift the pressure to the company, the leader, the church, or the pastor for making corrections and adjustments to change the low morale. In other words, when we have low morale, we shift the blame for the situation to someone or something outside of ourselves.

I have done a lot of thinking about who actually bears the responsibility for low morale, and have come to believe that morale is a personal issue. This does not mean that I believe that the work, church, or family system that one is operating within does not have some responsibility if the environment is dreadful; but it is more important for our maturity that we focus on our response to the dreadful environment. We are 100 percent responsible for our response. It does not help us if our response is to shift blame and play the role of victim.

I believe that my morale is my personal issue and is really not the issue of my employer, my wife, or anyone else. I am the pastor of the Mississippi Boulevard Christian Church and it would be irresponsible for me to dump my lack of morale on the congregation and staff. Whether I am happy or unhappy as the pastor is ultimately my own issue. My response to the circumstances and environment in which I find in myself is up to me. I have the ability to make different responses and choices to the situations that threaten my full participation. I have the power to change my response at any time. I can confront whatever is causing me unhappiness, make a decision to live with it if it cannot be changed, organize a boycott or protest based on personal responsibility, leave to make my own change, as well as a wide assortment of other creative responses. My morale is my personal response to the circumstances in which I place myself.

People use lack of morale as an excuse to withdraw support. People will not agree with a direction or a decision and they will allow it to affect their morale. Because they rationalize their behavior by saying that their morale is low, they will withdraw their financial, spiritual, or physical participation. They will not withdraw their membership, but they will withdraw the proper participation as a member. They will back away from their privilege to participate, while giving the illusion of participation. Jesus reminds us, "Let your 'Yes' be 'Yes' and your 'No,' 'No.'" I believe that we should either participate or not participate, and that illusion, make-believe, and membership on one's own terms are not the way of mature church membership.

There is probably not a pastor or leader reading this book who has not had some experience of threat, intimidation, or blackmail. Most pastors go through attendance boycotts, financial boycotts, and lack of spiritual support for the ministry in one form or another. Many people are in various stages of deciding on their level of commitment. But I am most interested in the blatant power plays, the obvious attempts to intimidate, and the visible outbursts of immaturity.

My friend from the Friedman class suggested that "anyone who, in the midst of the debate, states or even suggests that their participation with and support of the congregation is contingent on the decision reached should be disqualified from the debate." They should be disqualified for attempting to intimidate, to control the outcome. They should be disqualified for threatening "to take their ball and go home." They should lose the privilege to participate because they are not being truthful. They are not thinking about what is best for the church but what is best for themselves from their limited perspective. They are feigning the privilege of participation, but all the time abusing it through threats and intimidation. Jesus said, "Let your 'Yes' be 'Yes' and your 'No,' 'No.'" Jesus would say, "Make a decision to participate fully or not participate at all and live with the consequences." Membership on one's own terms is not the way of mature church membership. The true value of a member is his or her ability to hold to the privilege of participation even when he or she cannot convince the leadership that his or her perspective is correct.

Lesson 6: Separation Anxiety—John 6:60-66

THE PRIVILEGE OF PARTICIPATION IS VOLUNTARY AND SPIRIT-
LED SUCH THAT IF MEMBERS DECIDE THAT CONTRIBUTING TO
THE LIFE AND WORK OF THE CONGREGATION IS NO LONGER NEC-
ESSARY FOR THEM AND THEIR OBEDIENCE TO CHRIST, THE
CHURCH ACCEPTS THEIR DECISION AS THE WILL OF GOD AND
RELEASES THEM FROM THE PRIVILEGE OF PARTICIPATION, IN-
CLUDING FINANCIAL, SPIRITUAL, AND PHYSICAL SUPPORT OF
THE CONGREGATION.

*On hearing it, many of his disciples said, "This is a hard teach-
ing. Who can accept it?"*

*Aware that his disciples were grumbling about this, Jesus
said to them, "Does this offend you? What if you see the Son of
Man ascend to where he was before! The Spirit gives life; the
flesh counts for nothing. The words I have spoken to you are
spirit and they are life. Yet there are some of you who do not
believe." For Jesus had known from the beginning which of
them did not believe and who would betray him. He went on to
say, "This is why I told you that no one can come to me unless
the Father has enabled him."*

*From this time many of his disciples turned back and no
longer followed him.*

                                      —John 6:60-66

In my family of origin, we have been learning how to separate well. I remember how I separated from my father and mother's house. I grad-
uated from college, came home, and, with my brother, occupied the
same room that I had while growing up. I was dating my future wife
frequently. My brother, my sister, and I were only four years apart,
and we were all dating. As a result, there was not enough phone time
for me. I decided that I would put my own phone in the house since
I had a full-time job. Upon learning of my intentions, my father informed me that I could not put a phone line in his house. I protested
and declared that I was working and would pay for it. What difference would it make to him? He said that I fundamentally misunder-
stood that it was his house. Calm discussion escalated quickly and I
screamed and shouted until I went into my bedroom, slammed the

door, and hollered out to him, "I will get my own damn house and phone!" With that, my anger cascaded into streams of tears. Within two weeks I had an apartment. I left my parents' house.

Years later, as my I, my wife, and son did a similar separation dance at his leaving, I realized that my family had problems of separation anxiety. I did not know how to separate well from my parents' house, so we had to have a fight to separate. I could not reasonably discern that it was time to go and, therefore, plan to go. Though I knew it was time to go, going was so painful and so scary that I had to create conditions of anger and hostility to be able to go. That was what the tears were about in my bedroom. It was time to go, and I had great fear about whether I could make it, great uncertainty as to what awaited me out there, and great trepidation as to whether or not I was ready. My father gave me true, timely, and reliable information: it was his house, and I did not have the option to put a phone in. The purpose of the privilege of participation is not to make everyone feel good, but to help others make necessary choices. In my family's case, I did not know how to separate, so I got offended and fought.

I believe separation anxiety is what is going on in John 6:66. Jesus is in a theological debate with the religious professionals and clergy of the day. They ask him, "What must we do to do the works God requires?" (6:28). Jesus responds that the work of God is to believe in the one whom God has sent (Jesus). They ask for a miraculous sign to confirm that he is from God, such as the manna that their forefathers ate in the desert. Jesus declares, "I am the bread of life that has come down from heaven." They begin to grumble among themselves, asking how he can say he has come down from heaven when they know that he is Joseph the carpenter's son. Jesus says to them, "Unless you eat the flesh of the Son of Man and drink his blood, you have no life in you" (6:53). On hearing this, many of the disciples say, "This is a hard teaching. Who can accept it?" They are offended that he says they must eat his flesh and drink his blood. At this point many of the disciples turn away and no longer follow him. I believe that this probably is a case of separation anxiety.

There are times in life when we must make significant changes. I believe there is a place deep inside of us that knows that the next level of our growth requires that we move on. But being fearful of the unknown, we become anxious about separation, and our anxiety helps us to find something to be offended about. We have to create a serious disagreement in order to leave. That is what I believe is going on with the disciples. They wanted to leave and were not able to understand it, articulate it, or face it, so they got offended and found a cause for leaving.

Jesus says that they will be unable to come to him unless God enables them. Jesus suggests that everyone is not going to go all the way with him. There are some who God has given him who are to go all the way, but there are others who will become offended and leave. This happens every day in churches all over the world. People get offended and leave or get offended and threaten to leave. When the privilege of participation is extended, there will be some who will not accept it. True, reliable, and timely information will drive some to the point of being offended. The privilege of participation is not necessarily about all of us feeling good—it is about supplying the necessary information to people so that they can make the best choices for their lives.

The privilege of participation is voluntary and Spirit-led such that no one has to become offended to move on; or if they are offended and the offense is serious enough in the person's judgment, then it is okay to move on. Anxiety about separating is not necessary. I believe that there is pain in the separation, but that separation is a choice that people sometimes make. A mature person who separates owns the choice and assumes responsibility for it. When separation anxiety is poorly managed, the person who chooses to leave blames other people for forcing him or her out. The person channels the pain of leaving into anger directed at the leader or other persons in the church. The disciples in the John text blame Jesus for forcing them to leave. If a member receives true and reliable information but discerns, however, that God is not leading him or her to follow a certain direction, then it is okay if that member decides that contributing to the life and work of the congregation is no longer necessary for fulfilling his or her obedience to Christ.

I believe that sometimes separation is the will of God. I believe that God does mature some of us through separation. I believe that just as I had to leave my parents' house to develop fully into my own person, there are times in the Christian life when we must leave a church to grow up. Let us forgive all fights and offenses, understand them as separation anxiety, and accept separation as the will of God, releasing persons from the privilege of participation, including financial, spiritual, and physical support of the congregation.

I am sure that these are difficult words for the church. It is very hard for most churches to release members and very hard for members to leave. It helps me to understand that leaving is a natural and normal part of life. We must have some leavings to grow and become who God would have us be. It would be easier for us to become our full selves if we could bless and release people in their leaving and if the departing ones could bless and release the remaining church. Leaving a congregation is a natural and normal part of life—as much as death, the final leaving, is a natural and normal part of life. The privilege of participation includes people but, also, maturely releases people, too.

Lesson 7:
Mobilizing by Initiative—Acts 11:19-26

WHEN THE PRIVILEGE OF PARTICIPATION IS PRACTICED, LEADERSHIP IS DETERMINED NOT BY DOMINANCE STRUGGLES BUT BY THE WILLINGNESS OF INDIVIDUALS TO COME FORWARD AND TAKE RESPONSIBILITY FOR AREAS OF GROUP FUNCTIONING OR TAKE THE INITIATIVE IN DEVELOPING NEW ENDEAVORS.

News of [preaching the good news to Greeks] reached the ears of the church at Jerusalem, and they sent Barnabas to Antioch. When he arrived and saw the evidence of the grace of God, he was glad and encouraged them all to remain true to the Lord with all their hearts. He was a good man, full of the Holy Spirit and faith, and a great number of people were brought to the Lord.
Then Barnabas went to Tarsus to look for Saul, and when he found him, he brought him to Antioch. So for a whole year Barnabas and Saul met with the church and taught great numbers of people. The disciples were called Christians first at Antioch.
—Acts 11:22-26

In Acts 11:19-26, Barnabas encountered a volunteer initiative that spread the gospel to the Gentiles. A group of Jewish Greeks who believed in Jesus had been scattered because of the persecution of Stephen (7:54), and they were spreading the gospel as far as Phoenicia, Cyprus, and Antioch. Their mission efforts were primarily directed toward the Jews, but some of them from Cyrene and Cyprus took the initiative in Antioch to spread the gospel to the Gentiles as well, which was highly unusual. Great numbers of Jews and Gentiles were converted. Because of the mixture of Jews and Gentiles, however, the church looked different from any other church. It was a body of Jews and uncircumcised Gentiles meeting together for worship in fellowship with the Lord Jesus Christ.

When word of this reached the mother church in Jerusalem, tremendous concern developed over the mission work being out of control. The mother church decided to dispatch a delegate to do a fact-finding report and set things in order. Because Barnabas, whose nickname meant son of encouragement, was held in high esteem by all, he was the one delegated to go to Antioch.

When Barnabas arrived at Antioch, he was gladdened by what he saw there. He saw the privilege of participation. He saw the energy of responsibility and shared ownership. He did not see dominance struggles characterized by fights for power, control, resources, and territory. He did not see the insiders battling the outsiders. The text says that he saw "the grace of God." He was glad and he encouraged the people to stay true to the Lord with all their hearts. True to his name, he encouraged them, and an even greater number of people came to the Lord.

Barnabas was so impressed with Antioch that he went to Tarsus to look for Saul. Saul was the one who hunted and murdered Christians but met the Lord on the Damascus road and became a believer. Barnabas had supported Saul when there were suspicions about his conversion in Jerusalem (9:27). Barnabas knew of Saul's great ability, so he brought him to teach at Antioch. Barnabas and Saul met with the church and taught them for a whole year.

There was something special about this church at Antioch. It had unusual beginnings and an atmosphere of multi-ethnic fellowship and service to God. Outsiders noticed the ministry to the Gentiles and the fellowship of the Jews with Gentiles, which was beyond the normal bounds of what was permitted in Jerusalem. The Bible witnesses to it in recording that "the disciples were first called Christians at Antioch."

In my estimation, the church at Antioch practiced the privilege of participation. The privilege of participation is true, reliable, and timely, information that allows people to make the critical decisions of their lives. The privilege of participation bestows upon every individual the ability to function as an equal. Though there is hierarchy, the hierarchy serves to link equal and diverse levels of functioning rather than to enforce dominant-subordinate relationships. Where there are dominant-subordinate relationships, there are dominance struggles in the form of fights for power, control, resources, and territory. Once an individual, organization, or church moves into dominance struggles, a tremendous amount of time and energy is spent jockeying for position, and when people do that, the organization suffers from wasted energy and initiative. Productivity is curtailed because people do not divide responsibilities by giftedness and motivation but, rather, by power, control, and allegiance to a certain group, ideology, or party.

But when a group extends the privilege of participation to one another, as in Antioch, dominance struggles are minimized and a new energy is available. I believe that new energy looks like initiative in that the climate is created where motivated people can come forward and take responsibility for areas of group functioning. Opportunities for participation are created so people can get involved and offer their gifts, skills, and abilities without the politics of group loyalty being a prerequisite for participation. People can come forward and initiate new endeavors without hindrance or overreaching bureaucracy. The word *initiate* implies taking the first step—seeing a problem or concern and, rather than whining or complaining, taking up the challenge to do something about it. Initiative carries with it such positive words as *ingenuity, enthusiasm, enterprise, motivation, and ambition*. The church at Antioch teaches that when we extend the privilege of participation, people have the authority to initiate.

In some churches and organizations people cannot initiate any action because the underlying philosophy is that only a small group of people have the privilege of participation. In many churches, as Alan Nelson and Stan Toler say in *The Five Star Church*, the structure only allows a few trained professionals, or even a small group of volunteers and paid leaders, to generate ideas for constantly improving ministry.[11] In this kind of structure, a few people have the information (insiders) and, thereby, the privilege to participate and initiate. The majority of the people (outsiders) are excluded and passive. The outsiders complain that no one will let them in to participate. The insiders complain that there is no one to help them carry all the weight. The outsiders and insiders carry on a dominance struggle for power and control. In this struggle, much human, spiritual, and financial capital is lost.

The privilege of participation changes this paradigm. True, timely, and reliable information allows the insiders and outsiders to share responsibility, participation, and initiative. More and more volunteers in our culture are demanding the privilege of participation rather than tolerating dominant-subordinate struggles, probably because of the educational level of modern people. The more educated people are, the less they want to be told what to do. As a Christian education director that I worked with was fond of saying, "You drive cattle, but you involve people." People want to be meaningfully involved and less driven or commanded. I believe that if people are extended the privilege to participate, they will come forward and take responsibility for areas of group functioning or take initiative in developing new endeavors. Churches must make this very important shift if they want to maximize the contribution of current and future volunteers effectively.

Let me suggest some truths that undergird the privilege of participation and can help churches create a sense of ownership in their members.

1. People want true, reliable, and timely information about a problem, concern, responsibility, or task such that they can own it and see its fulfillment as their goal.
2. People are not interested in top-down, canned ideas and directives but want ownership in the process and product.
3. People want short-term, narrowly focused, and specifically defined tasks to accomplish. (I do not believe that people are too interested in committees that meet once a month for a two- or three-year period for the purpose of incremental change. Rather, they seem to like short-term and clearly defined projects that can make significant change if needed.)
4. People want to produce some action that has a tangible, visible product that can be delivered in a short period of time, and they want immediate feedback on the fruits of their labors.

When these truths are recognized, people tend to do a job well beyond expectations.

A shift is occurring in the ways people volunteer their time. Recruiting people to be on committees will not serve most of the membership. We will always have committees and committee work, but if we want to mobilize larger numbers of congregation members, it might be through what I call "initiatives." Initiatives are short-term team projects that address specific issues or concerns and that a group of self-motivated people conceive of and take responsibility for. Initiatives are specific, high-impact team projects that give a high degree of ownership to members of the congregation.

The believers at Antioch made the shift to the privilege of participation. They treated each other as equals and, therefore, avoided the dominance struggles that sap energy, strength, and creativity. They functioned with mutual responsibility and shared ownership. The result was that "a great number of people were brought to the Lord."

THE MATURE CHURCH LEADER

Assuming a person receives and possesses the Victorious Christian Life, gauges his or her personal maturity, successfully negotiates relationships with the body of believers, and becomes a mature church member, then he or she is ready for a position of church leadership. If church leadership is immature, then most often disagreement and dissent become chronic and complaining becomes regressive, hindering the church from accomplishing its mission and vision. Mature church leadership does not wipe out opposition or dissent but sets the framework for forthrightly handling differences of opinion that allows the church to maintain focus. The following principles represent core beliefs that shape and monitor a leader's commitment to maturity.

As a responsible first-born, I have spent most of my family-of-origin life in a position of leadership. Most of my adult life has been spent in a position of leadership in a local church congregation. In the attempt to fulfill my responsibility as a church leader faithfully, I have participated in seminars, workshops, and training sessions, and read many books, articles, and essays, on the subject of leadership. Most of them were concerned with how to teach certain habits that would make a leader more effective, such as time management, delegation, or vision casting. It was not until my work with Edwin Friedman that I began to understand the connection between leadership and maturity. Friedman taught that leadership has more to do with a leader's presence and being than with techniques and habits. Leadership has more to do with the emotional and spiritual maturity of the leader than the education and data available to the leader.

While most thinking on leadership focused on how to change the followers, Friedman focused on how leaders could change themselves. Friedman taught that it takes a great deal of courage to lead, and that leadership is connected to one's clarity, decisiveness, and "nerve." The title of his book, published posthumously, is *A Failure of Nerve: Leadership in the Age of the Quick Fix.*[1] From his vast experience, he believed that much of the leadership in this age of the quick fix operates from a "failure of nerve." He often called this kind of weak leader a "peacemonger."

> By [peacemonger] I mean a highly anxious risk avoider, someone who is more concerned with good feelings than with progress, someone whose life revolves around the axis of consensus, a "middler," someone who is so incapable of taking well-defined stands that their "disability" seems to be genetic, someone who treats conflict or anxiety like mustard gas—one whiff, on goes the emotional gas mask, and they flit. Such leaders are often "nice," if not charming.[2]

Peacemongering is an ingrained leadership style that usually takes more than attending a few seminars and learning conflict management techniques to overcome. It has to do with the nature of one's emotional maturity and functioning. It has to do with unresolved lessons about conflict that one has learned in one's emotional and family history. I know so much about this because I have struggled with peacemongering myself. I have known the panic and the anxiety that can come into my heart when I perceive that someone does not like my work or me, or when the inevitable conflict arises in a group, a work team, or in my home. I know the struggle of trying to maintain a position that I believe is right when people are mad and upset and shooting venom, negativity, and hostility my way. It takes a great deal of courage to deal with the "standing alone" and the conflict that is inevitable if you are going to lead anybody anywhere. This section is written to try to grapple with the kind of courage and inner nerve that it takes to truly stand alone and lead.

It takes such great courage to lead that I would like to approach this module in a very different manner than the previous modules. In Modules 1–3, I set forth a principle, established a scriptural text, and then explained the principle in light of that text. In Module 4, I will first tell a story that the lessons will refer back to. It will serve as a container for the leadership principles for this module. Story is the only form in which I can clearly articulate the courage, clarity, and nerve that it takes to lead. The story is fictional, but it draws on my experiences in many churches. The story is simply a teaching tool to help the reader experience the spiritual and emotional maturity that it takes to lead.

The Story

The rumors were almost unbearable to the ears of the chairperson of the Church Council. She kept hearing through the church grapevine that the beloved pastor and a member of the congregation were having a sexual affair. He had been the pastor of the church for more than fifteen years. Under his leadership the church had grown from ninety-five members to well over two thousand. He and his family were well-loved by the congregation and the community. The rumors persisted despite the deep love and affection between pastor and people. The rumors were so loud that she could barely hear him preach.

As she contemplated and prayed over what to do about the rumors, the phone rang. It was someone who announced herself as the close friend of a person who was in grievous pain because of the inappropriate actions of the pastor. The woman talked freely and authoritatively, giving names, dates, and details of the illicit relationship. She officially requested that the Church Council look into the matter. It was a rumor no longer. The chairperson's mind was spinning; she tried to come to terms with the fact that her pastor was being accused of sexual misconduct. But despite her shock and denial, the pastor was being accused, and the accusations could not be ignored. Her heart sank, and panic almost overcame her as she asked for the allegations in writing with signature affixed. The caller informed the chairperson that she would forward a letter to her after morning worship the next day. The caller hung up the phone, and the chairperson noticed herself shaking uncontrollably.

She did not sleep at all that night. She tossed and turned over what to do and what role she should play as the lay leader of the congregation. She tried to separate her feelings for her pastor from her responsibility to lead. But she gave that up and decided that it was *because of* her deep love for her pastor that she would truly try to lead in this time of crisis. She spent much of the night in prayer. She got up early to make two calls. She called the pastor and asked if he could meet her after morning worship. She called the vice chairperson of the council to arrange for an emergency meeting of the whole council for Sunday night. She then checked to see if the church had established any procedures for handling clergy misconduct. The church had not, so the chairperson knew that it was going to be even more difficult because there were no written policies and procedures in place. She prayed for the church, the pastor, the council, and herself in the coming days.

On Sunday morning, she did not want to go to church, and while she was there, she wanted to run out to avoid receiving the letter. But she remained and the letter was handed to her. She went to the prayer room and silently and calmly read it. There were the allegations, and there was a signature. She then went to the pastor's office to inform him that she had received a letter accusing him of sexual misconduct. The pastor denied the allegations and was shocked that anyone could accuse him falsely. She told the pastor that the Church Council would be meeting that evening to discuss the matter and that she preferred that he not be at the meeting so the council would have the full range of freedom necessary to deal with the matter fairly and equitably.

At the hastily called Church Council meeting, the chairperson read the letter out loud. The council sat in stunned silence. Prepared for their response, she and the vice chairperson announced that they had a plan. The chairperson and several members of the Personnel Committee would meet with the pastor to read the letter, hear his initial response, and offer spiritual support for him and his family. The vice chairperson and other Personnel Committee members would meet with the woman who wrote the letter to go over it, hear her initial response, and offer spiritual support for her. After hearing from both parties, the Church Council would get together, compare notes, and plan its next course of action.

What they did not plan was for someone to leak the information of the formal allegations, now spreading rapidly all over the church. The chairperson's phone rang off the hook. Many castigated the woman for either seducing the pastor, or bringing up false charges to discredit him. These people were vocal, angry, and extremely unkind. The pastor was a saint to them, and they were not going to allow anyone to tarnish his name. They declared to the chairperson that they would fight for the pastor to clear his name. It was obvious to them that the woman was a loose cannon and, therefore, all charges should be immediately dropped.

This crowd worried the chairperson. They assumed that anyone who did not stand with them did not love the pastor. The chairperson thought about how dangerous it was to equate love with blind loyalty. There were others who heard and immediately came to the defense of the woman. Still others were not sure of what to do or to think, so they simply prayed and waited.

The rumors became more and more exaggerated. Something had to be done. The Church Council met and decided to hold a congregational meeting to present the facts. At the meeting, the council reported that an official letter had been submitted accusing the pastor of ministerial misconduct in the form of a sexual affair. They declined to mention the woman's name. They explained that the Personnel Committee of the Church Council would conduct an investigation into the matter, and until all matters were resolved, the pastor would be asked to step down from all ministerial functions. The council expected that the matter would take three weeks to resolve, and the pastor would receive full salary and benefits in the interim. The Church Council clearly explained that these actions were not taken based on an assumption that the pastor was guilty, but to give everyone—the pastor, the woman, and the congregation—a chance for prayer, reflection, and sober consideration of the facts at the conclusion of the investigation.

Those who blamed the woman were outraged by the council's decision. They spoke openly about their love for the pastor. They detailed how he had been there for their families. He had baptized them, buried their dead, and married their children. His sermons had carried them through the most difficult times of their lives. He could not possibly have done any of the things that he was accused of. In fifteen years of ministry, there had not been any hint from him of this kind of behavior. They felt that the three-week suspension was totally unwarranted and argued vehemently against taking the pastor's wife and family through all of this.

Then the angry group made a bold and stunning preplanned move: it made a motion to dismiss the investigation of the Personnel Committee. The motion was immediately seconded, and someone called for the question. The motion sent the meeting reeling because no one had anticipated this action. The chairperson again panicked on the inside. Could they dismiss an investigation of the official leadership body? Could any justice be offered if they were not even willing to investigate the facts? What was it that God wanted done in this matter? Was it not an injustice to the pastor to have such an accusation leveled against him and not have it resolved? How did it help the pastor to have such an unresolved cloud over his ministry? Did not the woman deserve to have her accusation taken seriously? The chairperson loved the pastor too, but her devotion did not allow her to disregard a search for the facts. She needed the wisdom of the other Church Council members. While the matter was being hotly debated throughout the congregation, the chairperson decided to act fast. She could barely breathe as she interrupted the debating and said, "In the interest of unity and decency in the house of the Lord, please allow a fifteen-minute recess and cool-down period for prayer."

The council met in prayer. After praying, the chairperson offered the position that the motion was out of order on the grounds that in the exercise of its fiduciary responsibility, the Church Council had the right to control and restrict any activity that would run the risk of placing the church in a negative position with regard to a potential lawsuit. She reasoned that if the church ignored this complaint and did not investigate the allegations, the church was opening itself up for possible legal action. There was hesitance on the part of the Church Council to adopt her position, but no one had anything better to offer, so they agreed.

When the meeting was reconvened, the chairperson ruled the motion out of order based on the grounds she proposed to the council. She tried to explain that to ignore the charges would place the church in a difficult position that could result in legal action. At the conclusion of her words, pandemonium broke out. The Motion Party—people who supported the motion—was angry and hostile. The chairperson was accused of trying to run the pastor out. She tried to explain further with the help of other Church Council members who said that they loved the pastor too, but they were all shouted down. The voices of fairness said that if the pastor had not done anything wrong, then the facts would bear it out. There were those who sided with the Church Council, believing that the investigation should go forth. They were disturbed by the hostility and the lack of reasoning of the Motion Party. They rose up to attack the Motion Party. The meeting was out of control.

The chairperson announced that the Church Council would present itself for dialogue about the matter on the following Thursday evening. She said that due to the high emotional levels and the likelihood that the current discussion would only inflict more damage, the meeting would have to be adjourned. The Motion Party argued with her about whether she had the right to close the meeting. There were tears, anger, and shouting as she left the podium. The meeting was adjourned and the council left the room.

Between the phone calls and her own feelings of anxiety and stress, the chairperson did not sleep at all that night either. She lay awake wondering if she had done the right thing. Were there other options that she could have explored? She prayed and cried out to God for the courage to do the right thing.

The next evening there were meetings to discuss strategy. The Church Council met, and the group that made the motion met. The Motion Party felt angry, hurt, mistreated, and victimized. They felt that they had the right to have their motion voted on. They scrutinized the church constitution. They even recruited several members who were lawyers to make sure that they were interpreting the constitution correctly. They plotted to make their motion again, and if it was ruled out of order again, they would make another motion for the Church Council to be dismissed. They attempted to call the pastor to seek his advice. They threatened to withdraw their money and their membership. They began to poll people to see who was on their "side." They especially felt personal hostility for the council chairperson.

The Church Council meeting was difficult. Some council members had begun to second-guess the previous night's meeting and decisions. Maybe they should have let the vote go through and allowed the people to settle it. They were not comfortable with the amount of hostility and negative criticism they received. They reported receiving both phone calls of support and of total outrage. They reported that many people felt they had been denied their constitutional right to vote. They examined the church constitution. Should they reconsider their position? Should they recant? But they came to the fundamental position that justice and fairness meant the investigation had to go forth. The pastor and the woman had the right to a thorough, fair, and impartial investigation to determine the facts and resolve the matter. The facts would protect the pastor, the woman, and the church. They decided to stand by their decision, present themselves for dialogue, and discuss their position

At the Thursday meeting, they explained their position in writing and presented themselves for any and all to agree, disagree, and express their beliefs and opinions. The meeting started calmly, but rapidly descended into finger pointing, name calling, and blame. Some in what came to be called the Fairness Party made a motion to end all discussion and go forward with the investigation. The motion was seconded, and someone called for the question. But the Motion Party had no intention of allowing that motion to be voted on if their motion could not be voted on. They mockingly asked the chairperson to rule the second motion out of order. The meeting descended into total chaos.

The Motion Party had organized. They brought a constituency to the meeting and asked the constituency to rise as they read a prepared statement. It was obvious to them that they had the right, based on Article 2, Section 4 of the church constitution, to vote on their motion. They said that they wanted no more and no less than to follow the church constitution and *Robert's Rules of Order*. They demanded a vote. They threatened that if there were not a vote, they would resign from the congregation, withdrawing major financial support. The chairperson felt sick to her stomach as she noticed that almost one half of the room was standing. In her spirit, she said the dreaded words: *church split*. All that she knew to do was to offer the Motion Party a private meeting with the Church Council to see if there could be a resolution short of threats and intimidation. They were offended by her choice of the words *threats* and *intimidation*, but agreed to meet privately with the Church Council.

A meeting was held with the Motion Party, and they were intractable: either vote on their motion or they would withdraw financial support and possibly leave. They could not hear the arguments for fairness, justice, and a potential lawsuit. Under the guise of love for their pastor and his family, they were immovable. They had tied their loyalty to the pastor in the matter of the investigation, and they were not going to let it go.

The chairperson felt exhausted when she left the meeting. She was tired in a way that she had not experienced before. It was the tiredness of trying to convince people who refused to be convinced. They could meet for the next three weeks, and no movement would be made with this group. The chairperson wondered if the Motion Party knew the pastor was guilty, and in an effort to save his pastorate at the church, they were taking this position. She refused to meet with them again. They were going to have to do what they thought was best. Meeting with them would draw critical energy away from the Church Council's role to maintain justice and fairness for the entire church body.

When the Church Council met the next night, the chairperson sensed a shift in the air. The group had stood together to this point. They had called each other, talked over strategy, and though they disagreed in private, publicly they had maintained unity behind all decisions. At this meeting, several members expressed the outrage and anger that was being directed toward them personally. There were people in Sunday school classes and in fellowship groups who had been good friends with them, but who now turned their backs on them and shunned them. People who once spoke to them freely now ignored them totally. They could feel the church dividing and it scared them. Some of the council members reconsidered their position and wanted to allow the vote based on the hostility they were receiving.

They talked for four hours, agonizing and looking at the issue from all sides. They went back and forth from standing firm to recanting, from affirming their responsibility to lead to saying the people had the right to make the final decision. The chairperson stood firm in her position that justice and fairness required an investigation regardless of who was upset and who was going to leave the church. The council decided that all discussion would end at midnight when they would call for a vote. Each of the nine council members were to vote their conscience, and the majority would rule.

The vote came in at five to four to recant the council's position and allow the vote. The chairperson broke down and cried. It was not that the council had not voted her way, but it was the emotional pressure, the stress and anxiety of leadership that came down on her. It was the late nights, the phone calls, the conversations, not getting anything done at work because of conducting church business on the phone. It was the neglect of husband, family, and friends while trying to do the right thing. It was the pressure that all came out. Tears flowed freely from all. The chairperson said that she believed that the right and the fair thing was to conduct the investigation. She loved the pastor, but love does not mean ignoring the facts. She said that she intended to love him regardless of what happened. From her position the investigation was the right thing. But the Church Council had put it in the hands of the church and the church would now have to decide. She would abide by the decision of the church

The Church Council convened a meeting and informed the Motion and Fairness Parties that they would allow the motion to be voted on by the congregation. They explained their position and gave the congregation the authority to make its own decision. The Fairness Party objected vehemently. They were angry and hostile, but the chairperson prevailed on them to allow the vote to go through. The Church Council had prepared everything. According to the constitution, it took a simple majority to confirm a decision. The vote was to be by ballot. The ballots would be counted, and the totals would be given to the chairperson.

The chairperson implored the church's prayer warriors to have a time of prayer. They prayed for forty-five minutes before the vote. Then it was time for the vote. The voice of the chairperson cracked as she read the totals. The motion to dismiss the investigation was carried, 249 to 225. The Motion Party clapped and shouted for joy. The chairperson was sick. It took all of her strength to adjourn the meeting. She was devastated, but she could not let that be seen. She shook a few hands, hugged a few people, and left as fast as she could. More tears came. Council members and friends called to comfort and lament, but the tears flowed all night.

The pastor was in the pulpit the next Sunday and the Motion Party was there in big numbers. Several critical families in the Fairness Party were missing from worship. The chairperson was taken to the hospital with chest pains. Under the advice of her husband and doctors, she resigned her position as chairperson of the council. And the first order of business for the new chairperson of the Church Council was a lawsuit issued by the attorney of the woman who made the initial allegation.

Lesson 1:
Prayer as the Vehicle to Clarity— Matt. 14:22-23

LEADERSHIP IS THE SPIRITUAL PROCESS OF DISCERNING WHAT ONE BELIEVES (CLARITY), ACTING ON THAT BELIEF IN THE PUBLIC ARENA (DECISIVENESS), AND STANDING BEHIND THAT ACTION DESPITE THE VARIED RESPONSES OF PEOPLE (COURAGE).

Immediately Jesus made the disciples get into the boat and go on ahead of him to the other side, while he dismissed the crowd. After he had dismissed them, he went up on a mountainside by himself to pray. When evening came, he was there alone . . .

—Matt. 14:22-23

In the story, the chairperson of the Church Council demonstrated excellence in all three of the critical areas of leadership: clarity, decisiveness, and courage. Many people judge leadership based on whether or not the leader achieves his or her exact and desired outcome. From my perspective, true leadership takes a position based on principle and establishes the baseline a group must use for making its decision. Friedman taught that the leader is not responsible for the group: the leader is only responsible for the position of leadership within the group. The leader is not responsible for what the group believes, but is responsible for shaping a position of belief that helps the group discern what it believes. The leader is responsible for discerning what he or she believes, acting on that belief in the public arena, and standing up for that belief and action despite the affirmative or negative responses of the group.

The first step in the process of true leadership is achieving clarity. Clarity is the ability to decide what you believe in the midst of complex and conflicting issues and concerns. Clarity is a spiritual process, often discerned in prayer and solitude when one comes to know what one believes. In our story, the chairperson had to decide what she believed. When faced with accusations of sexual misconduct by her pastor, she consulted with God in prayer, searched herself and her own soul, and chose justice and fairness as her guiding principles through the crisis. As she thoughtfully worked through the tension, she came to believe that she loved both the pastor and the woman who made the accusations, and that love meant being fair and just to both of them. She was clear. As a leader, she was clear about what she believed and established her position. The overall church did not agree with her position, but that was fine. She provided a position from which the church could shape and define its position. That is leadership.

Many will agree with me and then ask, "How do you come to this kind of clarity?" First, we must admit that it takes many years of knowledge and experience to know what one believes. Friedman believed that it is not until well in our sixties that we truly come to know what we believe. But he also said that if you do not start trying to figure it out at twenty-five, you won't get there by sixty. Second, I believe one of the chief ways to come into clarity is through prayer. One of the things that cannot be denied about Jesus, regardless of one's theological perspective, is that he prayed. Jesus prayed often, early, late, before big decisions, and after big decisions. Jesus prayed at all times and in all places. Mark 1:35 states that very early in the morning, while it was still dark, Jesus left the house and went to the solitary place to pray. In Luke 6:12, Jesus prayed all night, and after praying all night, he chose his disciples. In Matt. 14:23, he prayed all day long before walking to the disciples on the water. While Jesus was praying in Luke 3:21 at his baptism, the heavens opened up and the Holy Spirit descended on him as a dove. We find account after account of Jesus in prayer. Prayer functioned as an avenue of clarity for him.

Prayer brings such clarity because it is in prayer that one hears the voice of God. I remember when I was studying with Friedman that a discussion took place in which someone described a desperate situation in ministry. Usually Friedman would offer insight, family theory, or some form of challenge in humor, but this time, after deep reflection, he said, "Get your Bible and go to the sanctuary!" His response stunned and bothered me. The more I thought about it, the more it bothered me and so I called him and asked him what he meant. He said to me, "It really does come down to getting your Bible and going to the sanctuary." He explained that it came down to one's sense of call, and the sanctuary and the Bible were the places where one clarified one's call. He said the preacher must answer these fundamental questions in prayer: What did God tell me to do? Where did God tell me to go? Sometimes, despite all the leadership theory and technique, all of the theological training and intellectual sophistication, it comes down to clarifying in prayer your mission and purpose. For many it means a time of sojourn in the solitary and lonely places in order to hear from God. Maybe that is why Jesus spent so much time in the wilderness and the mountains and the deserted places. He understood how essential it was for his clarity to hear from God.

When I teach this principle people often ask me if God speaks in an audible voice. I say to people that if I slow my life down enough, if I get quiet enough, and if I can calm down enough to wait, sometimes there comes screaming from within me a voice. And I know that it is not my voice. I know that it is the voice of God. Sometimes it is loud, sometimes it is quiet, but I know it is not my voice. How do I know that it is the voice of God? Because it often contains more wisdom than I know in and of myself. Sometimes it fits the pieces all together in ways I had not even begun to conceive. Sometimes I will lie down at night after wrestling with something that has exhausted every ounce of my strength and in the middle of the night from out of nowhere, when I am supposed to be asleep, the direction, the truth, or the vision comes. Sometimes when I am preparing my sermons, there is an insight, a leading, a prick of the heart, a gentle push to find something that I studied long ago, like a book that I have not thought of in years. Sometimes God speaks the vision and I know it. Someone once said that holy ground is the place where there is no uncertainty. Holy ground is the place of clarity.

Lesson 2: Decisiveness Is Faith at Work— James 2:14-17

LEADERSHIP IS THE SPIRITUAL PROCESS OF DISCERNING WHAT ONE BELIEVES (CLARITY), ACTING ON THAT BELIEF IN THE PUB-LIC ARENA (DECISIVENESS), AND STANDING BEHIND THAT ACTION DESPITE THE VARIED RESPONSES OF PEOPLE (COURAGE).

What good is it, my brothers, if a man claims to have faith but has no deeds? Can such faith save him? Suppose a brother or sister is without clothes and daily food. If one of you says to him, "Go, I wish you well; keep warm and well fed," but does nothing about his physical needs, what good is it? In the same way, faith by itself, if it is not accompanied by action, is dead.

—*James 2:14-17*

As wonderful as clarity is, it is not enough in and of itself. In the story, if the chairperson had been clear, but kept her clarity private, then there would have been a void in the church's leadership. She would have been weak and unable to help the church through the crisis. When the surprise motion to end the investigation hit the floor of the congregation, she moved from clarity to decisiveness, ruling the motion out of order. Clarity that moves to decisiveness is leadership. Our discussion is not about whether the content of her clarity and decisiveness was right or wrong, or whether she was right to rule the motion out of order. I am not discussing morality or procedural questions here. I am discussing the practice of leadership. She was a good leader because her clarity said that the church should stand for fairness and justice and she was willing to be decisive, applying her clarity in the public arena.

Recently I traveled with a friend to South Africa to interview several pastors for a publication that we were working on. We met with many pastors across the racial and denominational spectrum of South African churches. I was impressed with how many of them were speaking the same language. Most pastors suggested that poverty is the main problem facing postapartheid South Africa and postcolonial Africa. Because of poverty and the perception of hopelessness and helplessness that often go with it, there is a lack of food, education, sanitation, medical treatment, medicine, disease control, and disease prevention.

The South African pastors spoke a reality—Walter Wink's "natal alienation," which I mentioned earlier in Module 2. The pastors passionately said that the church must aggressively move from spiritual piety to actually changing the conditions of poverty in response to poverty and natal alienation. Several pastors talked about programs and businesses, and education and training intended to bring about what they called the "African Renaissance," but they were all honest about the fact that only a portion of the South African church was involved in the struggle to overcome apartheid. Other parts of the church were private and pietistic, with an almost totally otherworldly spiritual agenda. But all the churches of goodwill are faced with the prospect of moving beyond the past to uplift the nation's poor. It was encouraging to hear about such creative and powerful leadership. These bold and visionary pastors encouraged me.

As I listened to them, I was struck by how similar their work was to mine since, as an African American pastor, I too am faced with ministry to the poor. I realize that not everyone holding this book works with people who are alienated at birth, but beyond issues of race, class, sex, and gender, the struggle for all leaders is the same: to discover what we deeply believe and then put ourselves on the line for it in public. The South African pastors were saying that the church has to go public. The church has to move beyond the stained glass windows and the beautiful liturgy to touch the concrete and material needs of people. Leadership is discerning what you believe and then being decisive, which is to act out one's belief in the public arena.

Being decisive is a public process. It often involves a decision that must be made, an issue that must be faced, or a challenge that must be met. Often, decisiveness must be enacted in the context of competing ideas, philosophies, emotions, individuals, or groups. In the arena of this competition, a person must land somewhere. A decision must be made; a stand must be taken. The leader must be decisive. The leader must act out his or her belief in the public arena.

The root of the word *decisive* is *decidere*, which means "to cut off." When we must decide something we are forced to cut something: a competing idea, philosophy, emotion, or business deal. Many of us have the tendency to want to make everyone happy, to have it all, and to be in possession of both sides. But life has a way of forcing a choice. It is when a choice is demanded and we refuse to make the choice that we are indecisive. To be decisive is to make the decision to cut based on one's clarity. Often we are indecisive because we do not know what we believe; other times we know what we believe, but we are afraid. A true leader must be decisive.

James 2:14-17 teaches about the perils of having faith but not being decisive and acting on it. These verses teach us that we can say that we have faith; we can make an intellectual assent to faith, but if we do not have action that flows logically from our faith, then our faith is dead. The writer says that if our brother or our sister is hungry and naked, and we send them home with a blessing, spiritual saying, song, or Bible verse but do not give them things that are needful to them, then we are lacking in faith. If faith is real, it affects how we behave in the public arena. If the church will support an otherworldly, private, and pietistic spiritual agenda while people do not have food and clothing, then the faith of the church is dead. This makes no difference whether the church is in Africa, America, or anywhere else. Faith without works is dead. The writer of James suggests that faith is decisive in much the same way that these South African pastors are establishing that their faith must be decisive. Faith without a public ministry is dead. Clarity and faith without decisiveness are dead.

Lesson 3: The Courage to Lead

LEADERSHIP IS THE SPIRITUAL PROCESS OF DISCERNING WHAT
ONE BELIEVES (CLARITY), ACTING ON THAT BELIEF IN THE PUB-
LIC ARENA (DECISIVENESS), AND STANDING BEHIND THAT ACTION
DESPITE THE VARIED RESPONSES OF PEOPLE (COURAGE).

After you have enacted clarity and decisiveness, you must face the inevitable response from people, that is, agreement, disagreement, indifference, and other responses. Whatever action you take or do not take, there will be wide and varied responses from people. Some will affirm the decision or nondecision, and some will not affirm it. Some will think that you are a genius, and others will think that you are an idiot. Some will think that you are moving with deepest sincerity and following

God's lead, and others will suspect your motives and intentions of being purely self-serving. Many will be indifferent as long as the decision or nondecision minimally affects their lives. So the last, and possibly the most difficult, aspect of leadership is staying connected to the people and maintaining your clarity and decisiveness in the face of their varied responses.

Staying connected to people is such an important part of leadership that I want to be very specific about what it means. Staying connected means emotional contact with all the important people in a conflict or a dispute, especially those perceived as "difficult." It is easy to maintain clarity and decisiveness if the leadership disconnects, cutting off contact with the difficult people. But the mature leader stays in touch will all sides while maintaining clarity and decisiveness.

Friedman taught that staying connected was one of the "keys of the kingdom." The leader that did not stay connected was "asking for it down the line." He would say that if the leader and leadership fought with people in meetings, then the leaders had not prepared the ground, making it difficult, if not impossible, to stay connected.

Preparing the ground involves staying in touch and staying connected with people. Friedman taught that instead of getting away from difficult people or groups, leaders should view each relationship as an opportunity for developing greater maturity.

For the good of the church, the leader must must maintain clarity and decisiveness, which sometimes means standing alone. He or she must stay connected to people but stand independent of the various responses of people. The leader must have a prayerful, reasoned, and well-thought-out position independent of factions, politics, or the personal feelings of individuals. The leader must stay connected to the entire group, but maintain clarity and decisiveness in the face of the diverse responses of people. This standing alone for the good of the church is what I define as courage.

Courage is the ability to maintain your position when you believe you are right, even when people are saying that you are wrong. Courage is the ability to change your position when you know you are wrong, even though people think that you are right. Courage is the ability to discern your position based on an internal guidance system, rather than always checking for signals from the ever-shifting opinion polls, so you can determine what you will believe and how you will act. Courage does not mean that you never change your position or always change your position. Courage means that you do not change your position to please people, acquiesce based on tactics of fear and intimidation, or give in to make the group or other people feel better. On the other hand, courage is not remaining rigid to show everyone that you are in charge, or to be inflexible because of the false and prideful idea that changing one's position shows weakness. Courage means that you hold fast to your position, change your position, or compromise on your position based on your inner discernment of principle alone. Courage is the ability to maintain a position based on an internal thermostat, rather than the outside thermometer of people.

As this lesson explores courage, it will examine how to maintain clarity and decisiveness in the midst of the varied responses of people. The lesson will present five principles, illustrated through the Response to Leadership Chart (on pages 74–75) that applies to both the courageous leader and the courageous follower.

Positions 1 and 2

ANY TIME A LEADER OR LEADERSHIP GROUP MAKES A CLEAR DECISION, SOME MEMBERS WILL BE UNABLE TO RESIST THE TEMPTATION TO DEFINE THEMSELVES AS VICTIMS OF THE DECISION ("IT WAS WIN/LOSE, AND WE LOST.").

The story at the beginning of this module is illustrative of this universal principle: any time a leader or leadership group makes a decision, some in the group are unable to resist the temptation to define themselves as victims of the decision. By ruling out of order the motion to dismiss the investigation, the Church Council took the position that an investigation was the fair and just thing to do. The Church Council functioned with clarity and decisiveness. In response to their leadership, the Motion Party connected loyalty to the pastor with the position of closing the investigation and defined themselves as victims of the Church Council's decision.

To define oneself as a victim of a decision is to cast the relationships that flow from that decision into the arena of dominant-subordinate struggles. The moment persons define themselves as victims of a decision they give up power and place themselves in the subordinate position. From the subordinate position, it looks like the dominator won, and the subordinate lost. From the subordinate position, it is very difficult to see an issue or concern in a larger context.

Response to Leadership Chart

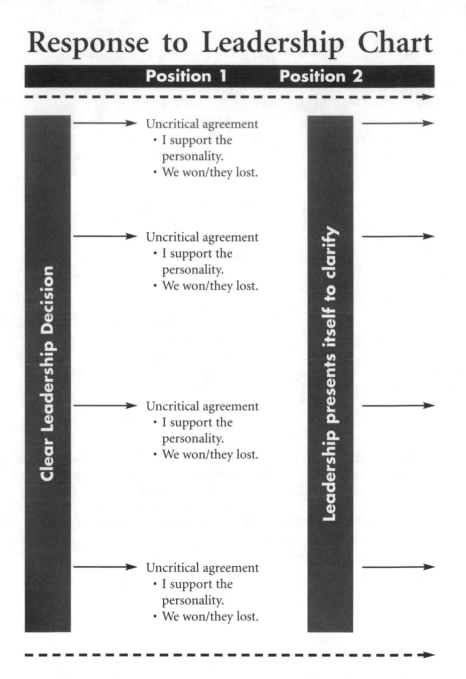

Position 1   Position 2

Clear Leadership Decision

Leadership presents itself to clarify

Uncritical agreement
• I support the personality.
• We won/they lost.

Uncritical agreement
• I support the personality.
• We won/they lost.

Uncritical agreement
• I support the personality.
• We won/they lost.

Uncritical agreement
• I support the personality.
• We won/they lost.

Position 3	Position 4	Position 5

- →

Leadership tries to move the group from personality and win/lose to win/win	Leadership caters to uncritical support	Personality-based leadership
Leadership tries to move the group from personality and win/lose to win/win	Leadership caters to uncritical support	Burned out leadership
Hardened victims	*Nonconstitutional processes to get rid of leadership*	*Church split, court fights, etc.*
Leadership dialogues to discover place of mutual agreement • Win/win principles	Leadership accepts principled opposition	Principle-based leadership
On principle work for new leadership	*Constitutional process for new leadership*	*New Leader*
Affirms leadership based on principles	Leadership accepts principled support	Principle-based leadership

- →

The big picture might be what is best for the group as a whole or what the majority of the group sees as its best interest. But from the subordinate perspective, it is difficult to perceive oneself as part of the whole. From the victim position, it is difficult to see what options one has outside the dominant-subordinate paradigm and perceive oneself as an equal. It is only when we see ourselves as equals that we can explore the full range of options that we have in response to any decision or action. We always have a vast array of nonvictim responses to any action or decision. We are never to define ourselves as a victim of an action or decision because if we do, we give away our power and place ourselves in the subordinate position in the midst of dominant struggles.

I heard it said once that pain is inevitable in life, but misery is optional. Pain is what we experience in response to some of the actions and decisions that we are faced with in this world. Misery is the sum total of our unhealthy victim responses to the pain. We will have pain, but that pain does not have to descend into misery. Our response determines whether it is simply pain or misery. When we define ourselves as victims, we place ourselves in the subordinate position and misery is a part of our condition.

Some would respond that if a decision is wrong, unfair, or discriminatory to a person or group, then that person or group is a victim of that decision. It is not that people do not have the right to disagree with leadership decisions. People have the right to agree, disagree, or be indifferent to any leadership decision. People have the right to start out in disagreement and move to agreement or start out in agreement and move to disagreement. But people do not have the right to define themselves as victims of a decision. As humans, we tend to believe that the critical factor in relationships is whether or not people agree or disagree with us. I want to suggest that what is more critical than the agreement or disagreement is how persons function within their positions. If agreement or disagreement is based on principle rather than emotional arguments, such as defining oneself as a victim, then usually whatever position is taken serves the relationship. Principled agreement or disagreement serves to help congregations make informed decisions. But when disagreement or agreement is based on victim and dominant-subordinate struggles, it is harmful to congregational life. I am suggesting that for every clear decision there is a minimum of four responses, which are either helpful or harmful to the church (see Positions 1 and 3):

Response 1: Uncritical Agreement. This response will agree with the decision, but agreement is based on emotional arguments, such as "I always support the pastor." Usually, people who take this position will uncritically support the personality or personalities in leadership regardless of the principles involved. Those who respond this way see agreement as loyalty and will support the leader even if the leader is dead wrong. Often, they will see any opposition as persecution of the leadership, and will respond with defensive zeal. In the extreme form, they are out to win for the leader, and if they are not careful, they will shape the discussion in terms of winning and losing. Often, after the opposition is rebuffed, they will point the finger and say, "We won, and they lost." The Motion Party in our story represented this group. They gave uncritical support and agreement to the pastor and sought to defeat the investigation based on their belief that it smeared the name of the pastor.

Response 2: Uncritical Disagreement. This response is disagreement with the decision, but it is based on emotional arguments such as "I never liked the chairperson of the Church Council anyway," or "They are hiding something and I know it." Usually, people who take this position will uncritically oppose the decision based on personal issues, regardless of the principles involved. In the extreme form, they are against the decision because of who made it or who recommended it. They shape an opinion based on some emotionally held opinion. In years of being a pastor, I have discovered that there are people who uncritically oppose whatever the pastor puts forth. Whatever the pastor proposes is automatically and summarily rejected, and the opposite is automatically proposed. For the Motion Party, the pastor's image is an emotionally held concern, and when a decision violates their emotional perspective, they define themselves as victims of the decision. If the majority does not agree with their assessment, then they will decide, "They won, and we lost." They will blame, point fingers, and point out flaws in the voting process.

Response 3: Principled Disagreement. This response disagrees with the decision, but the disagreement is based on principles. You will often hear an "I" statement. For example, if someone disagreed with the council's decision, he or she might say, "I disagree with the council's position that the Personnel Committee of our church should conduct the investigation alone because I believe that we should secure strong outside participation from the national church. First of all, the national church has experience in this kind of matter, and second, it can insure objectivity and impartiality in the investigation." In this statement, the speaker takes personal responsibility for his or her position. One will not cast blame, point fingers, or set things up as win/lose propositions. We must always keep our responsibility for our decisions in the forefront rather than give our power away. This position is a more thoughtful one and it allows people who have different opinions to disagree without getting into dominant-subordinate struggles.

Response 4: Principled Agreement. This response is similar to the principled disagreement response. You will often hear personal responsibility in the form of an "I" statement in this response as well. A person who agrees with the Church Council's position on principle might say, "I agree with the decision to conduct an investigation because the truth will serve the church, the pastor, and the woman who made these allegations. I do not believe that ignoring this, covering it up, or pretending it never happened helps anyone. The truth will allow all of us to move forward and make the best decisions for our lives." This is a thoughtful position based on agreement with the principles behind the decision, and it allows people who have different opinions to disagree without getting into dominant-subordinate struggles.

These four responses to leadership decisions can be found in almost every congregation. The most important thing is not whether one agrees or disagrees, but how one functions with one's agreement or disagreement. Uncritical agreement and disagreement allow emotional arguments to control the discussion, which results in a win/lose framework for everyone. Win/lose frameworks are always about divisive factions, secrets, information leaks, church fights, church splits, and other unresolved conflicts. When we move to maturity, our agreement or disagreement is based on principle rather than emotional arguments.

The factors that allow many people in churches, families, and workplaces to agree and disagree uncritically and thereby engage in emotional arguments rather than principled ones, are: (1) lack of factual information, (2) lack of clear boundaries, and (3) lack of respect fora person's right to make decisions within the context of his or her boundaries.

Years of church experience have taught me that many churches do not facilitate the flow of factual information throughout the entire organization. First, as we stated earlier, people act based on the information that they receive, and most churches must admit that they have not been diligent in communicating factual information. Second, most churches are very unclear about boundaries.

Boundaries answer questions like, "What am I responsible for? What decisions can I make or not make with regard to what I am responsible for? What authority do I have?" Many churches operate with a lack of clarity. When roles and boundaries are unclear, they can become anyone's. Third, if we are not clear, how can a person's right to make decisions be respected within the context of his or her roles and boundaries? With such a lack of clarity, people second-guess decisions on faulty and emotional information rather than state principles on which they disagree. Instead of respecting a person's right to make a decision in his or her area of responsibility, those who are affected by the decision will define themselves as its victims.

But principled agreement or disagreement is more likely to be found in a system that has factual information, clarity with regard to roles and boundaries, and respect for the decisions of people within their boundaries. I have found it extremely helpful in the midst of emotional and intense discussions to ask the question, "What are the facts? Who has the right to the final say in this matter that we are discussing?" I often say, "Let's discuss the matter and give input, but then let the person who has the responsibility in this area make the final decision."

Position 2

When the leadership of a congregation regularly presents itself to the congregation and clearly announces that it is willing to speak to any member who feels victimized, the leadership takes the initial step for dialogue. From that point on, it is up to the person (victim) to seize the opportunity.

It is absolutely predictable that if a leader or leadership body makes a decision some people will define themselves as victims of the decision.

People are entitled to clarification of the decision by a leader and leadership body. By clarification of the decision, I mean the setting forth of the facts and reasons behind a particular decision. I do not believe that the leadership should pass the buck, run, hide, or shroud itself in secrecy and mystery. Leaders owe the congregation a responsible, factual, and thoughtful discussion of any decision. The people have this right because of the privilege of participation.

In the story, it was necessary from the standpoint of the privilege of participation for the chairperson to offer another meeting night when the council would clarify and discuss its decision to rule the motion out of order. There are some people who, no matter how fact-based a decision is and how many times it is discussed, will not accept it. Therefore, I do not mean meeting and discussing ad nauseam, because I have learned in leadership that there is a point beyond which discussion is not fruitful. The decision must be accepted or rejected, and a person must exercise his or her options in response to the decision. But I fundamentally believe that leaders owe people a reasonable, timely, and factual explanation. I believe the leadership should offer the privilege of participation regularly and willingly.

The leadership has a responsibility to present itself regularly to the congregation and speak to any members who feel victimized. Any member who feels overlooked, mistreated, or otherwise abused has a right to dialogue. This does not mean that the leadership will agree with the member's sense of victimization but that people deserve reasoned and principled discussion of their concerns. The leadership must explain itself, but not necessarily until everyone is satisfied, because only rarely is everyone satisfied. The leaders must, however, offer the opportunity for dialogue.

Church leadership has a responsibility to present itself, and church membership has a responsibility to seize the opportunity for dialogue. I once had a member who came to me after a congregational meeting and complained that the meeting was not fair. When I asked why it was not fair, she told me that people were intimidated by my presence, and were not able to speak up and say how they really felt. I said to her that I presented myself for dialogue and did not prevent anyone from speaking. It seemed to me that it was their responsibility to seize the opportunity. She said that people were afraid to disagree with their minister. I acknowledged that there were some people who probably found it difficult to disagree with their spiritual leader, but I felt we could teach a new paradigm. It was not whether one agreed or disagreed with the spiritual leader but how one functioned within the agreement or disagreement. I told her that we must teach people to agree or disagree on principle and not emotional arguments. She ignored my comments and then volunteered to speak for those whom she said could not speak for themselves. I said to her that I believe that people should speak for themselves. If she would be willing to arrange the meeting with them, it would be all right with me if she tried to assist them in saying what they thought and felt, but no human being should speak for another human being.

I believe people gain maturity when they have the opportunity to speak for themselves. When the leadership fulfills its responsibility and offers the opportunity for dialogue, then any member who feels victimized, overlooked, or otherwise abused must seize the opportunity.

In connection to my belief that people should speak for themselves, I have taken the position that I do not read anonymous letters. I will address any concern that people are willing to put their name on. If people do not have the courage to put their name on what they believe, then I will not waste my time reading it. When we allow people to get away with not putting their name on what they believe, we cater to and foster immaturity in people. Once I received a letter that said, "Based on your decision, many members will be leaving." The persons signed their names. I called them and said, "I do not respond to threats and intimidation. Rather than tell me that many are leaving, tell me that you are leaving. I respect that and I will talk to you about that." I believe people should speak for themselves. Allowing anonymous letters and nameless accusations is the abuse of leadership.

Positions 3 and 4

ANY LEADERSHIP BODY OR CONGREGATION THAT ADAPTS TO
THOSE MEMBERS WHO CANNOT RESIST DEFINING THEMSELVES
AS VICTIMS PUTS ITSELF AT A DISADVANTAGE IN CONFRONTING
CHALLENGES THAT ARE INEVITABLY PART OF ACHIEVING ITS
MISSION.

Typically, after the leadership presents itself for clarification, most of the time is spent with uncritical agreement people. But if we are not careful, we will spend tremendous amounts of energy trying to keep people from defining themselves as victims. In other words, we can spend tremendous amounts of time and energy trying to refute, change, or make people give up or move out of their emotional arguments and win/lose positions. People do not give up their emotional arguments very easily and without personal growth.

I have tried many things to move people away from their emotional arguments. I have spent a lot of time trying to refute each emotional argument point by point. I have tried befriending people—getting to know them and letting them get to know me. I have tried giving them more responsibility and putting them in leadership positions. I have tried ignoring them and disregarding their comments. I have tried caving in to them, compromising with them, pacifying them, and even standing up to them. What is certain is that the more you attempt to move people from their posture of victim, the more you will burn yourself out. People must give up their emotional arguments on their own.

I have learned that burnout is rarely simply related to how much work one does. Burnout is a relational issue. *We do not get burned out when we do the work that is legitimately and appropriately ours; we get burned out doing the work of others.* For example, Friedman relates that a scientific experiment was done with monkeys. As long as a monkey was put in charge of getting food for himself, no matter how hard the monkey worked, he never got an ulcer. But as soon as the monkey was in charge of getting food for the other monkeys, he showed early stages of an ulcer. The message is obvious: we burn out getting food for people who are able to get food for themselves. People who have defined themselves as victims attempt to manipulate others into getting food for them. If the church is busy getting food for those who define themselves as victims of leadership decisions, then the church will never achieve its mission.

But rather than face the reality that catering to victims will take us off our mission, we try to do the personal growth work that people can only do for themselves. When people have defined themselves as victims, we rush in and try to persuade them not to feel that way; we run in and try to rescue them. Say someone announces that he or she is going to leave the church because of a decision that was made regarding a particular issue. If we rush in and try to convince the person to stay, or go to the leadership and convince them to change their minds so that the person can stay, or if the leadership changes its mind so the person can stay, we are guaranteeing burned out leadership. We are guaranteeing that the church will never achieve its mission because much of the energy of the organization will continue to

be spent pandering to immature people. People have the right to respond to any decision. We cannot keep people from being victims.
But we still have the right and the responsibility not to allow the victims to stop or hinder the rest of the church from accomplishing its
vision.

Very often in leadership, if we are not careful, we attempt to do
the work of other people. I once was the leader of a church that was
having a building campaign. I and another person spent untold
hours getting the church through the building process to the point
that our families were totally neglected. We covered every base, we
spoke to every person that was not giving. I preached every sermon,
I raised every offering, and he handled every detail and made every
meeting. When we came to the point of the celebration and dedica-
tion of the building, I was absolutely burned out and did not enjoy
the celebration at all. My partner, the building chairperson, took a
sabbatical from church work, and it was two years before he could
become actively involved as a volunteer in the life of the church
again. Was it anyone's fault but mine and his? We had overfunc-
tioned. I could not accept the fact that the members might not have
wanted a building as soon as I did. We did the work of other people
and burned out as a result.

The temptation of leadership is to adapt to those who define
themselves as victims in order to "keep the peace" or remain "one
happy family." The temptation is to give in and let them have their
way because they often rattle the chains the longest and the loudest.
But any group that adapts and caves in to victims puts itself at a disadvantage for accomplishing its mission. The victim people will
consume so much time and energy that the leadership will not be
able to address real concerns.

I have even noticed that when victims discover that they cannot
throw the leadership off track, and the leadership and the rest of the
group decide to move forward beyond the victims' concerns, they
will even feel justified in secretly plotting to get rid of the leadership.
At Position 4, I have placed an arrow where the victims become what
I have called "hardened victims." Hardened victims are so locked into
their emotional arguments that if the leader will not see their point
of view, they will plot to get rid of him or her and get someone in
who will do things their way. This results in major win/lose church
conflicts, such as church fights, church splits, court fights, and ter-
minations. But there is a fair and equitable way to bring about a

change in leadership; it is healthier for the congregation to follow the route of principled disagreement.

If you follow the route of principled disagreement, you will see that the leadership negotiates principles with the principled disagreement crowd. If there is dialogue around principles, then it might be possible to find common ground and move forward. Mature leadership accepts, dialogues, and reasons with principled disagreement. Usually, both sides are working on a win/win principle. And when a win/win outcome is not possible, the principled leadership can see that there is a principled way to get new leadership. That group will follow the constitution to get new leadership that will more closely align itself with the group's principles. This, in theory, happens each time there is an election in the United States. For leaders, the principled disagreement crowd does not take anywhere near as much energy to deal with as the uncritical disagreement crowd. The difference is that the leadership is not trying to move the principled disagreement crowd from the position of victim.

I have also spent a significant amount of time trying to get the uncritical agreement crowd to move to principled agreement. I believe the leader is always on surer footing if the basis of people's functioning is principle rather than emotional arguments. Just as leaders sometimes cave in to the victims, they can also cave in to their uncritical support. Leaders become lazy or are in a hurry and do not do the necessary preparation, legwork, fact gathering, and information processing to help the congregation to support a decision. Rather than use a fair process that includes as many people as possible, the leader attempts to ride on the uncritical support of people. The leader is positioning himself or herself in a win/lose arena, gambling that he or she will always be able to keep enough uncritical supporters to win the debate or discussion. Usually, the leadership engages in emotional arguments to cover the lack of preparation and diligence. People agree or disagree based on emotional arguments such as personality. This is one of the sure ways to guarantee and perpetuate personality-driven leadership. I believe that true leadership is based on principle rather than win/lose discussions.

Finally, there is the group that any mature leader wishes there were thousands more members of, and that is the principled agreement crowd. There is an ease of relationship and thinking that operates when we agree on principle. People in the principled agreement crowd have, out of their relationship with God, developed important principles and beliefs that form the basis for actions in their lives. When they find these principles in the vision or in the leader they support them based on principled agreement. Loyalty and human wisdom are not the only reasons they support a decision. These can be factors, but the most important point is that the decision represents well-thought-out principles.

This means that to deal with a decision, the principled agreement people go first to their relationship with God. In the context of that relationship with God, they discern where they are headed in their own spiritual life. People must work out a personal vision for their own life if they are to support a leader's decision based on principle. People who operate out of principled agreement support the decision or the leadership because the principles behind the decision resonate with their own personal standards and vision.

I believe the principled disagreement crowd operates in the same manner as the principled agreement crowd. It just so happens that they disagree with the principles behind the decision and cannot support it. Their disagreement is not a loyalty issue, but results from the decision not lining up with their standards and their vision. It is from the principled agreement and disagreement crowds that maturity most often operates in the Body. When agreement or disagreement are operating from the level of principle, then the Body can maintain its focus to accomplish its vision.

Position 5

THE LEADER IS NOT RESPONSIBLE FOR THE ENTIRE CHURCH
BUT ONLY FOR THE POSITION OF LEADERSHIP.

It has taken me many years and numerous trials, tribulations, defeats, victories, and glorious blessings to come to the final piece of thinking and belief expressed in this module. I have played the role of savior. I have also played the role of victim. I have been the pastor of a group of eighty-seven people with no cash and no building. I have also been the pastor of an 8,000-member congregation with plenty of space, facilities, and tradition. When I synthesize my years of experience and learning, I distill them down to one truth that sums it all up for me: the leader is not responsible for the entire church but only for the position of leadership. The leader is only responsible for staying connected and being clear, decisive, and courageous. The church must respond to the clarity, decisiveness, and courage of the leader, and how the church responds determines the level of leadership it receives. If the church responds with maturity, it receives good leadership. If the church responds with victimlike immaturity, it gets immature leadership. It is impossible to distinguish the functioning of leaders from the people who produce and respond to the leader. The mature functioning of the people has much to do with the kind of mature leader they produce. It is also true that the mature functioning of the leader has much to do with the kind of people he or she produces, but we will close this module with the mature leader as the final piece of thinking.

The leadership model that I am setting forth looks very different from the forms of leadership that we are most acquainted with. The leader does not tell people what to do, force his or her will on a group, blame others, abdicate leadership by not taking a position, scapegoat the opposition, or carry all the weight and responsibility of the congregation. *The leader provides a vision for others to evaluate.* The leader attempts to use his or her own clarity effectively to help the congregation discover what it believes. The leader does not try to change others; the leader tries to be clear about what he or she believes and what he or she is willing to risk based on those beliefs. The leader takes up the hard work of being clear, decisive, and courageous, while staying connected.

This is a very different way of thinking about leadership. My model stands against manipulation, coercion, deceit, tricks, secrets, half-truths, misinformation, scapegoating, and dictatorship in order to move forward an agenda or a program of a leader or leadership body. It opposes the hireling expression of leadership in all of its weak and noncourageous forms, such as letting the congregation shape the vision alone, being afraid of the congregation and therefore a slave to its opinions, and avoiding conflict because the leader only says or does what he or she is paid to say or do—what Friedman calls "peacemongering."

The Mature Leader

The model of spiritual maturity resists the kind of thinking that suggests that the pastor is solely responsible for the church and the souls of people in the church, which is described in Heb. 13:17: "Obey your leaders and submit to their authority. They keep watch over you as men [and women] who must give an account. Obey them so that their work will be a joy, not a burden, for that would be of no advantage to you."

Although the Pastoral Epistles and the Letters of Paul gave frequent admonitions to leaders for proper dealings with their followers, there is very little counsel in the New Testament concerning the way that people should treat their leaders. The Hebrews verse spoke directly to the people as to how they should regard leadership. It made the case that the responsibility of leaders was very great. They were responsible for watching over even the souls of the people. They had to give an account of the spiritual, material, and physical welfare of the people. Since leaders were responsible for the outcome, it seemed reasonable to allow them to be the ones who decided how things would be done. The leader was therefore obliged to enforce discipline and call attention to spiritual faults, inappropriate behavior, and doctrinal impurity in order to maintain the health, integrity, and welfare of the community. Some of the people to whom this text was originally addressed probably did not like the church discipline and may not have been willing to "be subject" to their leaders. This kind of insubordinate behavior made the job of the leader difficult and unpleasant, which was damaging to the welfare of the group. The writer of Hebrews admonished the people to obey the leaders and therefore make the leaders' work a joy. It cannot be disputed that the normative and effective biblical model of church leadership was one in which leaders were responsible for the church and the souls of the people.

In our time, I have heard recitations of this biblical model over and over again; pastors say to people and people say to pastors that the pastor is responsible for the church and the souls of the congregation. As a result, many of the members hold the leader responsible for regulating the well-being of the congregation. The downside of this control is the tremendous level of stress that it places on the leader. The leader ends up with massive amounts of stress because being responsible for others engages the dominant-subordinate struggles talked about extensively in Modules 3 and 4.

First, it is difficult to be responsible for the church and the souls of the people when the church, in response to twenty-first-century culture, has dictated decreasing levels of authority to the minister. Historically, the minister was one of the most educated and most respected members of the community. The minister held tremendous spiritual and moral influence and authority on behalf of God, which benefited the church and the community. But given flourishing secularization, increasing educational levels, and individuals' social, political, and economic sophistication, people now look more on themselves as authority figures and less on the minister as such. It is extremely stressful to be responsible for people if one does not have the authority to go with the responsibility.

Second, the leader ends up with massive amounts of stress because many people understand the mandate from Hebrews to mean that they should place themselves in the subordinate position. Whenever people place themselves in the subordinate position, leadership by cult-of-personality is engaged. The result is that people underfunction and the leader overfunctions. In many instances, the people are passive while the leader—and a few people surrounding the leader—make the decisions and carry the weight of the ministry. We have already discussed the major pitfalls in this kind of relationship system between the pastor and the people.

Again, I do not want to imply that there is no rank or hierarchy. It is clear that the leader is the leader, but equality is one of the basic beliefs of hierarchy. In a functional hierarchy, information links people in order to accomplish the task rather than to determine our rank or importance. I advocate functional hierarchy because when you are responsible for anything other than your own behavior and your own soul, it adds gargantuan levels of stress to your life. When the leader feels responsible for people, the leader will attempt to move people out of the victim posture, and the result is that it will burn out the leadership. The leader is responsible for his or her own behavior and soul in the position of leadership. The leader extends to the people the privilege of participation and functions with the people as an equal.

The leader's responsibility is to be clear, decisive, and courageous and thereby provide leadership to the group. The leader will shepherd—teach, preach, live out mature Christian beliefs and principles—and guard against heresy. The shepherd will perform pastoral duties such as weddings and funerals, while always sharing the responsibility and empowering others. It is tremendously stressful to be singularly responsible for all the functions of the shepherd. It is the shepherd's responsibility not to do all the functions, but to ensure that all the functions are carried out.

When we look at the shepherd's role from this perspective, we have a leader who is not responsible for the group, but responsible for the position of leadership. It is the responsibility of leadership to ensure that the shepherding function is carried out. The leader will shepherd his or her own soul and present a clear, decisive, and courageous vision for others to evaluate. This does not mean that the group will do what the leader wants or believes; it means that the group is responsible for its behavior and decisions. Whatever decision the group makes in response to leadership is not the leader's ultimate concern.

A friend of mine read *They Call Me Coach*, the story of John Wooden, the legendary coach of the University of California at Los Angeles (UCLA), who won nine out of ten NCAA championships— an unprecedented record. My friend was impressed that in thirty-five years of coaching, Wooden never mentioned the word *winning*. Wooden never encouraged the players to look at the scoreboard during the game. He stressed that they should focus on the fundamentals, play as a team, and do it all with character. If they could walk off the court with the feeling that they left everything out on the court, played as a team, and carried themselves with character, then they were winners regardless of the scoreboard. If they did these three critical things, the scoreboard would take care of itself.

Coach Wooden's thinking about the scoreboard is exactly my thinking about leadership. To worry about the decision the group makes is to worry about "winning." If the leader plays as a team member (extending the privilege of participation), and functions out of personal maturity (like Wooden), then the leader has provided leadership regardless of what the people decide. If the leader extends the privilege of participation and functions out of personal maturity, then the leader has provided leadership regardless of what the congregation decides. The decisions of the people will take care of themselves.

Let's return to our story. Did the Church Council cave in to pressure? Did the Church Council adjust its position on principle, or did they adjust to lower the heat in the kitchen and please people? I do know is that the chairperson was clear, decisive, and courageous. She could have manipulated others to support her position, but instead she gave the group the responsibility for its decision. She provided the privilege of participation. If the council collectively shifted and caved in to the people, it was the people's responsibility. After the debate, the council decided to let the congregation vote on the issue. The leader cannot be responsible for the decision of the group but must provide leadership so the group can make a decision. Once the facts are presented people make the decision that they assume is in their best interests. She was not responsible for the behavior of the group; she was responsible for the position of leadership.

When the matter came to the floor of the congregation, the congregation voted to close the investigation. Was this a good decision? Should the leader of the council have imposed her will? Should the leader rescue the group, or must people bear the consequences of their choices? Most often, people get the level of leadership they deserve. If people disregard facts and clear thinking and support distortions, cover-ups, and other inappropriate actions and behavior, they deserve the level of leadership they get.

It might also be true that leaders deserve the level of people they lead. It might be that over time, the people can rise no higher in their maturity than that of their leader. If the leadership caters to the uncritical agreement crowd, then the church will have personality-based leadership. If the leadership caters to the victims in an attempt to move them out of the victim posture, then the church will get ineffective, burned-out leadership. If the leadership accepts principled disagreement and principled agreement, then the leadership will be based on maturity. Mature leadership will preserve health and balance in the congregational body.

EPILOGUE

If the church is to be effective and relevant for God-centered ministry in the twenty-first century, it needs to be spiritually mature. Maturity can release the most creative, imaginative, and dynamic thinkers to set the agenda for present and future challenges, rather than spend their energy on the most dependent people—the chronic complainers and the regressive thinkers. Maturity does not wipe out dissent and disagreement, but handles them directly and forthrightly so the church can stay on track to accomplish its mission.

I am aware that as we talk about maturity, we are talking about change because in order to mature, we must change. Change and growth, which is the positive response to change, is very difficult for most of us to deal with. It is the fact that change and resistance go beyond all the rational and logical boundaries that make leadership so difficult. But as leaders this is exactly our call—to persevere through resistance to help the Body to grow and change.

In response to difficulty, many leaders feel drained and depressed from time to time. It goes with the territory, and as Kirk Byron Jones says, "Such is the cost of real caring."[1] In one of my down moments, a talk with a friend helped me. This is the summary of our conversation:

> Congregational leadership is a hard job. It is a test of faith. Can you give up your need for it to get better? Can you live in this crucible? Can you accept that it is a hard job and probably will not get any easier? If you give up the need for it to get easier, it might not be so hard. Can it be okay that it is so hard?

This thinking helped me begin to truly accept that it is okay that leadership is so hard. Nothing was wrong with me, and nothing was wrong with the church. We were just engaged in the normal and natural process of growing and changing. Meeting challenges is a hard job, but it is the only road to maturity. You are getting stronger and stronger. You are becoming mature.

Congregational leadership is a healing modality. I have learned how to treat transitions and crises as opportunities for growth, rather than as hostile environments that victimize and require escape. Based on critical thinking, action, and reflection on the principles in this book, I continue to increase my spiritual and personal maturity. Congregational leadership, despite resistance, is fundamentally a healing modality. It really is okay that leadership is so hard.

THE STATEMENT OF HEALTH, BALANCE, AND MATURITY IN CONGREGATIONAL LIFE

Module 1:
The Call to the Victorious Christian Life

The church is the place where people can hear Jesus Christ urge them to a live a VCL.

Jesus says that the way leading to destruction is broad and easy, and there are many who find it. The way that leads to a VCL is narrow and hard, and there are few who find it and possess it.

The basis of a VCL is not freedom as a social, economic, or political category but freedom as an inner spiritual reality and identity that is based on a saving relationship with Christ.

We are 100 percent responsible for maintaining the freedom of a VCL based on how we respond to the events, situations, and circumstances that occur in our lives.

One who has the freedom of a VCL grants to others the freedom to be 100 percent responsible for how they respond to the events, situations, and circumstances of their lives.

Module 2:
The Mature Self

Following the original sin of disobedience, the most appealing, most prevalent, and most frequently nonresisted temptation is to play the role of victim.

Following the sin of playing victim, the most appealing, most prevalent, and most frequently nonresisted temptation is to play the role of savior.

Every victim needs a savior, and every savior needs a victim, and victim and savior together do a dance of immaturity that is destructive to both lives.

Any statement that begins with "He/she/you/it made me . . ." reflects the temptation to play victim.

Any statement that begins with "He/she/they cannot do . . . for themselves" reflects the temptation to play savior.

One's ability to allow others to experience pain and consequences for themselves is the key to avoiding the posture of savior.

The ability to tolerate and handle one's own pain constructively is the key to avoiding the posture of victim.

Module 3:
The Mature Church Member

The most significant opportunity and benefit a congregation gives to a member is the privilege of participation, which is the responsibility and right to contribute to the work of the congregation.

The ultimate value of members and leaders to the congregation is not judged by the orthodoxy of their beliefs, the size of their contributions, or the length of their service, but by how well they uphold the principle of the privilege of participation.

The most grievous abuse of the privilege of participation is trafficking in secrets, that is, rumors, gossip, information leaks, third-party information, anonymous letters, and church intelligence and espionage.

The direct opposite of the privilege of participation is resolving church and family conflicts through scapegoating.

The withdrawal of financial, spiritual, or physical participation and support, but not membership, to protest a pastoral, leadership, or congregational decision is an abuse of the privilege of participation.

The privilege of participation is voluntary and Spirit-led such that if members decide that contributing to the life and work of the congregation is no longer necessary for them and their obedience to Christ, the church accepts their decision as the will of God and releases them from the privilege of participation, including financial, spiritual, and physical support of the congregation.

When the privilege of participation is practiced, leadership is determined not by dominance struggles but by the willingness of individuals to come forward and take responsibility for areas of group functioning or take the initiative in developing new endeavors.

Module 4:
The Mature Church Leader

Leadership is the spiritual process of discerning what one believes (clarity), acting on that belief in the public arena (decisiveness), and standing behind that action despite the varied responses of people (courage).

Any time a leader or leadership group makes a clear decision, some members will be unable to resist the temptation to define themselves as victims of the decision ("It was win/lose, and I lost.").

When the leadership of a congregation regularly presents itself to the congregation and clearly announces that it is willing to speak to any member who feels victimized, the leadership takes the initial step for dialogue. From that point on, it is up to the person (victim) to seize the opportunity.

Any leadership body or congregation that adapts to those members who cannot resist defining themselves as victims puts itself at a disadvantage in confronting challenges that are inevitably part of achieving its mission.

The leader is not responsible for the entire church but only for the position of leadership.

NOTES

Introduction
1. Edwin H. Friedman, *Generation to Generation: Family Process in Church and Synagogue* (New York: Guilford Press, 1985).

Module 1: The Call to the Victorious Christian Life
1. David Schnarch, *Passionate Marriage: Love, Sex, and Intimacy in Emotionally Committed Relationships* (New York: Henry Holt Company, 1998) 51.

2. E. R. Dodd, *The Greeks and the Irrational* (Berkeley: University of California Press, 1951).

Module 2: The Mature Self
1. Walter Wink, *Engaging the Powers: Discernment and Resistance in a World of Domination* (Minneapolis: Fortress Press, 1992), 82.

2. Edwin H. Friedman, in an oral presentation at the Center for Family Process, (Bethesda, Md., January 1994).

Module 3: The Mature Church Member
1. Stephanie J. Ferrera, "Lessons from Nature on Leadership" (paper presented at the Conference on Organizations, Georgetown Family Center, Washington, D.C., April 22–23, 1995), 12.

2. Ibid.

3. Ibid.

4. Rev. Dr. Alise Barrymore, in a conversation at New Faith Baptist Church (Matteson, Ill.).

5. Peter Titelman, ed., *The Therapist's Own Family: Toward the Differentiation of Self* (Northvale, N.J.: Jason Aronson, Inc., 1992), 297.

6. Walter Wink, *Engaging the Powers: Discernment and Resistance in a World of Domination* (Minneapolis: Fortress Press, 1992).

7. Ibid., 144.

8. Ibid., 146.

9. Ibid., 148.

10. Ibid.

11. Stan Toler and Alan Nelson, *The Five-Star Church: Helping Your Church Provide the Highest Level of Service to God and His People* (Ventura, Calif.: Regal Books, 1999), 98.

Module 4: The Mature Church Leader

1. Edwin H. Friedman, *A Failure of Nerve: Leadership in the Age of the Quick Fix,* edited by Edward W. Beal and Margaret M. Tread-well (Bethesda, Md.: Edwin Friedman Estate/Trust, 1999).

2. Ibid., 12.

Epilogue

1. Kirk Byron Jones, *Rest in the Storm: Self-Care Strategies for Clergy and Other Caregivers* (Valley Forge, Penn.: Judson Press, 2001), ix.